THE ART OF THE ARCHITECT

TRIGLYPH
BOOKS

THE ART OF THE ARCHITECT

Michael G. Imber

TRIGLYPH
BOOKS

Contents

Foreword

By Clive Aslet

This book is an architect's manifesto for hand drawing. As technology offers ever more aids to the design process, this fundamental skill might look old-fashioned, even obsolete. The author's contention is that drawing and sketching have a role that can never be replaced by the computer, because they convey an individual human being's response to the architectural challenge being addressed. Call it 'inspiration' at the beginning of the design journey, or the 'soul of the building' when construction has been completed. It is the interaction between eye, hand, and paper which creates the magic, or to put it another way, instills spiritual meaning.

There may be other ways of doing this, on screen for example. But screens are notoriously difficult to use in the field, whether under intense sunlight or pouring rain. Besides, hand drawing is a quicker means of recording the essence of a place, in all its nuances of light and shade. A sketch simplifies and edits: it necessarily filters what the artist-architect sees, and communicates a personal vision. It is alive with the spirit of the person who did it. Even the lucky accidents of serendipity can be absorbed into the sketch, prompting new lines of thought. All this informs the architectural result.

Michael makes a compelling and passionate case for this art based on his own dedication to drawing and watercolours over the years. Not shown in this book are finished projects by Michael G. Imber, Architects, except as they appear in renderings, often exceptionally accomplished. Anyone acquainted with the work will know that they seem almost to grow out of the ground on which they stand. There is a set office-style dictating how they look. The idiom in which they are designed reflects their setting. Consequently, they are so much at ease with their environment that they might always have been intended to sit there. In achieving this, drawing makes a significant contribution. Michael sketches the landscape around the site on his first visit. This not only produces a record of what it is like, but is a process of study. When you draw a thing you have to look at it hard. You internalise colors, shapes, forms. When you return to the drawing, you can remember

Traveling and learning through drawing are part of the tradition of becoming an architect. Cass Gilbert (1859-1934), *Church of St. Francis, Assisi*, 1898. Watercolor and pencil on paper, 18 ¼″ x 11 ⅞″.

the play of the light, the smell of the meadow grass, and the sound of the cicadas. A photo on a smartphone is done in an instant, but sketching takes time. That time is all-important to analysing the features around you.

The resulting sketch may have aesthetic merit: as can be seen from this book, the drawings and watercolours produced at the different stages of the design process can be beautiful to look at. In a presentation which is intended to seduce the eyes of a client, this may be a primary aim. Usually, though, it is a secondary consequence of an activity which has a less elevated purpose. Architectural drawings give information. In this, the pen is still, in some instances, mightier than the computer. How much quicker it is to take out a sketchbook and convey an idea to a builder by means of a rapid sketch than to attempt the same thing on a laptop. Clients have always been dazzled by an architect who can conjure a three-dimensional idea out of a few pencil strokes on a scrap of wastepaper. Their imaginations are fired. They are not being offered the finished article but a vision which is as yet sufficiently broad for them to participate in the development. Even hardened businessmen can respond to the poetry of pen and wash.

The Metropolitan Museum of Art in New York owns a drawing of the façade of Strasbourg Cathedral drawn in the 1260s. It raises the question of how many other architectural drawings were made in the Middle Ages because very few survive. We can assume they were rare, not least because of the cost of the parchment made from animal skins on which they were drawn. The Strasbourg drawing shows the pattern of crockets, arcades, and tracery which cover one wall of the cathedral. It is a flat, diagrammatic representation. A revolution came in the Renaissance when it became possible to show buildings on paper, drawn in plan, section, elevation, and perspective. Three-dimensions could be rendered in two, in a manner that could be easily carried from one place to another. Clients, who would otherwise have required a scale model to visualize what their architect was talking about, could now see the intended shape of their commission at a glance. Architects developed their own visual language, from the cool and precise washes of a Sir Christopher Wren, to the staccato dots and dashes of pen combined with sepia washes that was Robert Adam's style. One advantage of making drawings was that they could be shown to craftsmen. Thus building became more than a purely local activity, which relied on the skills of whichever craftsmen happened to be on the spot. It could be more cerebral, displaying the design capabilities of the person in charge. Gradually a word emerged to describe that person: architect.

In the early days, architects could also be artists, masons, or gentleman amateurs. In the course of the 18th century, their role became increasingly specialised. In the 19th century, architecture came to look increasingly like a profession, whose members had technical expertise. Was it, though, an art or a science? The debate continues even today, although in the 21st century it is obvious that architects have to know a huge amount of subjects that are not at all related to art to do their job: engineering, IT, building regulations, accountancy, law. With so many calls on their time the design element may only get done out of office hours, at the very beginning or end of the day. This makes

Right: A quick thumbnail sketch drawn during a journey across Texas with Yale students to study vernacular architecture. The sketch was done in less than two minutes: a fleeting reaction to the environment. Michael G. Imber, *Morris Ranch Schoolhouse, Fredericksburg*. Graphite sketch.

hand sketching and drawing all the more important. It is a reminder of architecture's roots in buildings like Strasbourg cathedral. Just as the masons who cut the stones used their eyes and hands, so does the architect using a sketchbook. Like riding a horse or playing a musical instrument, it is an activity which connects the Now with the deep past.

Wall paintings on the walls of caves show that human beings have felt the urge to represent their surroundings since the earliest of times. In this book, Michael describes how the recording of the virgin American landscape was a fundamental part of nation building in the United States. In recent years, the world has become especially aware of the value of drawing as one of the activities that slows us down, gives time to think, concentrates on the local, and generally forms an antidote to our otherwise high-pressured, jet-setting lives. So people have always drawn and see a particular point in it today. May the profession hear Michael's plea for hand drawing to remain at the heart of architecture. This book, largely of his own wonderful drawings, demonstrates its continuing power.

Clive Aslet is visiting professor of Architecture at the University of Cambridge

Morris Ranch Schoolhouse, Fredericksburg

Preface

I have always seen architecture as a romantic profession. Historically known as the Mother of the Arts, or even the Mistress Art, architecture has, since ancient times, been conceived of as having a timeless place in our lives. She emerges from the deep past to look to the future. She expresses who we were, who we are, and who we wish to be. Over long epochs she has become a palimpsest of cultural overlays, layering meaning upon meaning. Architects are supposed to be visionaries, calling up images of what life might be like in an idealized future; yet we have also always built upon the foundations of our ancient civilization, seeking to understand the intricacies of those foundations as they run all the way to bedrock. This gives us a stable platform from which to reach higher and higher as we grasp the concepts of beauty, plumb the wonders of technology, and attempt to give new meaning to our built environments. Before we can do any of this, however, we must observe the world around us. Traditionally, this was best done through drawing. It enabled architects to look, record what they saw, internalize what they had drawn, and contemplate it. This enabled them to formulate new ideas and expressions.

Architecture and architectural practice have changed much since the second half of the 20th century. In the past, art and science were always forces to be weighed and kept in balance by the architect. Today, we have leaned hard into the science of building and away from art. The computer replaced the pencil as the primary means of expression in the profession. Architecture has become more technically driven, more future driven. For many architects today, sentiments of the past, such as beauty or nostalgia (a longing for that which we know), have become irrelevant to the outcome. This isn't the fault of the computer; it is a change in philosophy in how we look at building for the future. Yet because of the nature of the machines we use, architects have largely created a hermetically sealed process; solutions are reached, conceived, processed, and determined much as they might be in a lab—scientifically, rarely emotively.

Almost every architectural firm today, including my own, would say computers are essential to the processes of design and building. This book is not a judgment of the

This painting has had a profound effect on Michael throughout his career as it was the first watercolor he had seen used to illustrate contemporary architecture in an architectural journal. Given Michael's passion for both watercolor and architecture, it provided a moment of realization. Abdel-Wahed El-Wakil, *House of Hyrda*. Watercolor.

machine in architectural practice. Far from it. The computer has proven its capabilities as a tool in the modern office; it is here to stay, and is ever-evolving. Our powers of invention have been strengthened by the computer, not depleted. Yet, central to *The Art of the Architect* is a deeply felt belief that the one tool that architects have always had at their disposal to keep us connected to our environments, to our cultures, and to our humanity is hand drawing. We obtain a more profound understanding of the world as artists.

There are very specific requirements to becoming an architect: typically, five to seven years of school, followed by a minimum of three years of apprenticeship, every hour of which is formulated to give the architect all the tools necessary for modern practice, before taking the excruciating twenty-hour exam. Yet, of all the segments of hours necessary to pass this requirement, only one has the architect out in the field—construction observation. And today, not one segment requires hand-drawing or a knowledge of art.

My desire for this book is simply for it to illustrate the importance of field observation and of hand-drawing as a necessary skill of the architect, and to show that by drawing and painting, architects may continue to transform the world as artists, not merely as technicians. My hope is to re-inspire architects with the joy of observing and with the idea that by seeing, in particular, the landscapes in which we live we can reconnect our architecture to place, and to enrich our ideas for the creation of more rewarding environments for the future.

I do not intend to present an academic history of art or architectural drawing through the ages. As Edgar Payne says, 'The study of art is a lifetime matter'. My pursuit of art in architecture has been a lifetime's quest in search of knowledge through seeing. My observations are those of a practicing architect who has an interest in art and in history but, above all, several decades of experience as a designer and architect seeking to respond to the character, histories, and cultures of the locations in which I build. I see architecture and art as a continuum, and architecture and drawing as part of a living tradition connected to how those before us observed our world and formulated new ideas from those observations.

My recent teaching at Yale University School of Architecture brought me into direct contact with some highly talented students and has made me reflect on what entrants to the architectural profession need in order to truly see and understand the communities and landscapes in which they are to build as they move into their future careers as architects. Generally, my students had not spent much time hand-drawing or sketching, much less getting to know a thing or place empirically through drawing. The first day of studio they were given a sketchbook. As we were to begin a 1400 mile journey through Texas, they were told they were to fill its pages with buildings, materials, details, landscapes, trees and bushes, anything that was a response to where they were and what they saw. It didn't matter if they were good sketches or bad, they only had to draw. They

A scene of Venice painted at top speed during a late-night, jet-lag-stricken stroll. It is the action of making the sketch that matters, rather than the quality of the rendering. This serves as a reminder to Michael that architectural drawings need not be entirely accurate. Michael G. Imber, *Venice, Italy*. Watercolor.

thrived, and to many it was a revelation. They found it to be an engaging experience of both liberation and fulfillment. It is my hope that these students of architecture, as well as many others of this generation, find these tools as much a necessity in practice as I had discovered when I was a student, and it is my hope that they will continue to see the importance of architectural drawing and watercolor as a critical craft of the architect.

01

Art into Architecture

The Art of Seeing

"I am thinking therefore I exist"

René Descartes, *A Discourse on the Method*

I first learned to see like an artist on nature walks with my godmother, Aunt Margaret. She lived at the end of the old Galveston Highway, long ago abandoned since the bridge was washed out by a hurricane. Off her backyard were the remains of the oyster-shell road disappearing into the South Texas jungle. We would go on long, slow walks through this dark, foreboding wood, looking. She would point out orchids, alligator nests, birds: things you don't normally see if you aren't looking for them. Her studio was filled with paintings of the orchids she found there as well as old sailing ships she had imagined. She patiently taught me to draw. I would sit for hours as she painted, drawing dragons, and whales and the ships that hunted them. When I graduated from high school, she gave me my first watercolor kit. But by then, given my family had moved hundreds of miles away, I had to learn to use them on my own.

At architecture school, I rejected the popular medium of the time—colored markers—in favor of watercolors. Traditional drawing, or traditional architecture for that matter, wasn't considered in architectural programs in the 80s. But with the help of a few supportive professors I actively pursued both behind the scenes. Journals out of Europe, like *Tradition and Architecture*, gave me the inspiration I needed: beautiful watercolors by contemporary architects illustrating modern traditional buildings. I returned to these journals time and time again to emulate their techniques. Having done well in studio using watercolors, I would fume when I made a 'B' in rendering class because I used watercolor instead of markers.

Unknowingly, I had aligned myself with a long, indeed ancient, tradition of architectural drawing. It evolved from the era before television, before radio—when art, writing and storytelling were the mediums of culture. They conveyed our relationship with one another, the world around us, and the worlds beyond us. Today we live in a fast-paced

A birthday card painted by Michael's artistic Aunt Margaret who sparked his imagination as a young boy. She loved to draw flowers, but would amuse Michael by drawing sea monsters and other fantastic creatures with him. Aunt Margaret, *Sunflower*.

world driven by technology. At the center of this technology is our handheld device—the technological marvel of the phone. Phones can do just about anything, from sending messages to connecting us socially, checking our bank account, purchasing, mapping us somewhere. Integral to the phone is a digital camera capable of astounding results and we use it to take instant, high-quality photos of friends, ourselves, places, and things that have momentarily caught our attention. We routinely 'capture' thousands of images, effortlessly and with barely a second thought. Why sketch? Why go to the trouble of representing buildings and places on paper, using old-fashioned pencils and watercolors, when the digital alternatives are so handy?

This book attempts to answer these questions. It constitutes a heart-felt plea to architects to remember the origins of their art. The fundamentals of that art have not changed, despite the dichotomy that has haunted architects since the 19th century, summed up in the title of Richard Norman Shaw and Thomas Jackson's 1892 book, *Architecture, a Profession or an Art?*. Digital programs do many things that the great architects of the past could hardly dream of, and in my office they are an effective tool. But the soul of a building derives from the moment of conception, when a human mind pictures to itself a three-dimensional form—a leap of imagination, a leap of faith, which is then conveyed directly by the hand onto paper. This is the romance of our profession. It is this bringing of the "unseen"—the conceptual—into the physical, perceptual world that is the architect's hat-trick. Computer software is a wonderful tool, as familiar today as the old-fashioned T-square was of old. But the architects of the past did not expect their T-squares to generate ideas. Ideas arrived by a process that not even modern neuroscience can explain from the human brain. I do not say they came fully formed. They had to be developed by techniques such as the *esquisse* and *charrette* of the École des Beaux-Arts in Paris. These relied not on the divine spark of creation (and just as well, because how many geniuses are born per generation?) but on the practice of craft. Craft has always been humankind's way of empirically transforming the physical world, imbuing it with our own spirit of humanity: whether through iron, wood, stone, clay, paint, or even words. I fear that as the prevalence of simulation-based computer programs in the design process is undermining the role of the architect, we are losing the craft of the profession.

This book will not be focused on rendering or technical drawing, nor on fine art. It will describe the art of seeing, a different way of looking at the world and processing it, in order to build. Through drawing we make choices. We filter what we are seeing through our own perceptions of the world; what we choose to see is framed by our own beliefs, experiences, and prejudices. We attempt to represent the world through our own eyes and the act of doing so in turn shapes our ideas of the world. These processes, which are part and parcel of drawing, are key to the formation of that intangible spirit without which a building is dead. There is a danger that modern technology will create spaces that do not instinctively relate to human beings, having been generated by machines. However excellent and useful, cold lines on a computer screen do not have the emotional and cultural backstory conveyed instinctively—perhaps without the artist so much as knowing it—by brush or pencil. Spirit, hopes, dreams, love, fears, labors, stories, mythologies, meaning; none of these things can be calculated by machines but they may be implicit in the work of the human hand.

The skills associated with architectural drawing are now in danger of being lost, but they are essential to the creation of architecture that will serve, delight, inspire, and satisfy the people who use it. If architects, and particularly students of architecture, having turned the pages of this book then put it down and pick up a pencil and brushes, I shall have achieved my purpose.

Another example of Aunt Margaret's artwork painted on a piece of plywood that she beat with a hammer to create texture. It originally hung in Michael's childhood bedroom and has now found a home on the wall of his guest bedroom in Maine. Aunt Margaret, *Boat*.

Memory

Pictures are the loopholes of escape to the soul.

Sir John Gilbert, as quoted by Edgar Alwin Payne

On my first visit to the studio as Robert A. M. Stern Visiting Professor in Classical Architecture at Yale, I ensured that each student was given a sketchbook. The pages of these books would begin to be filled in while traveling in Texas (the site of their project) but continue in use during the course of their design work. On arrival in San Antonio, the students were picked up from the airport by bus and we drove directly to the historic Spanish Governor's Palace, our first stop. Within minutes of setting foot in Texas they found themselves sketching the historic courtyard of an 18th-century compound. This was the beginning of an odyssey across the Lone Star State: from San Antonio to the Rio Grande River on the border of Mexico, to the missions and presidios of South Texas, to the 19th-century forts that guarded against the Comanche attacks in the Texas Hill Country, to the high-desert plateau of Marfa in West Texas, and then on to El Paso.

The sketchbook wasn't merely an exercise in graphics but a way for the students to immerse themselves in the culture and landscape so that they would begin to understand the place on a deeper level—beyond the classroom exercises in cartography, and beyond a textbook understanding of a place for which they were to design for. Sketches weren't only meant to enhance the observation of the buildings they were studying, but to put the students in that place: to see the grain of the wood etched by wind over time, to feel the burning heat, and to smell the dust that carries with it generations of stories. Sketching was intended to inform them as architects of the many different architectural solutions that the varied cultures of Texas brought with them: different views on nature and on God, the contribution of native peoples, and the resources the land had to offer for building. A sketch was meant to understand the twisted tree under the intense Texas sun, the shade and shelter it provided, then to understand the contorted grain of the heavy lintel that was felled from such a tree and fashioned by hand to resist the gravity

Before undertaking a 1400-mile trip across Texas, all the students on Michael's 2022 course were given a sketchbook in which to record their impressions of the architectural sites encountered during their tour. The WPA Pavilion was built during the Great Depression, when the government created jobs for unemployed workers building park structures such as this. George Knight, *WPA Pavilion*. Associate Professor at Yale. Watercolor.

of the stone above it. Only by sketching the tree could you understand its journey, place, and purpose. It was meant to put the students in a place of true understanding.

Before our road trip, I had little idea of how radical my sketchbook-based program would appear. Until today, drawing has always been a part of an architect's education. For generations the École des Beaux-Arts in Paris trained architects alongside artists and sculptors in the skills of observation. Drawing was central to the education of each of them in their allied arts. It was not until the late 19th-century that American architects had access to this system. In the 1800s, architecture was barely formed as a profession and most of its architects had been imported from overseas. Among the different American cities in which a home-grown tradition of architecture developed, Boston stood out as the center of architectural drawing, as a loosely formed system of professional architects attempted to educate themselves on Western architecture and on their skills of drawing. Eventually, their collaboration led to the formation of two of the earliest architectural schools in the U.S.—M.I.T. in 1865 and the Boston Architectural College in 1889. By then, several other architectural schools had begun to form in America shaping the unique architecture of a nation to its own cultural landscape. Much of this pedagogy has disappeared from academic teaching. Drawing— the mainstay of architecture for centuries—is no longer taught, depriving students of what ought to be an invaluable creative tool.

Above: A building in Gonzales, Texas painted by a young Yale student working towards a Masters degree in architecture. Claudia Carle, '22 Yale Student. Watercolor.

Right: The presence of the yucca tree is the only indication that this is the same WPA Pavilion that Knight painted (previous page). The contrast in style shows the diversity of form offered by different impressions. Michael G. Imber, *WPA Pavilion*. Graphite sketch, 16 ½" x 5 ¼".

As a visiting professor at Yale, I was faced for the first time with the modern pedagogy of architectural school in which drawing by hand plays a minor or secondary role. This isn't necessarily a Modernist approach to education: most well-known Modernists from the 20th century valued drawing in many respects. This is a change in our tools, what the *New York Times* once called 'The 40lb. Pencil'—the computer. Like most students anywhere, my graduate students at Yale had their formative education and training on computers. Although students were expected to take a hand-drawing course as an elective, drawing was not commonly integrated into the design process, nor was it considered as an academic research tool for observing the places they design for. The course, a graduate-level design studio, required them to understand the local conditions in order to respond with a solution that was fitting to the place in which they were designing. Cartography (or a researched mapping of cultural influences) was something they were well adept at creating as an underlying basis for the knowledge and understanding of a place. Drawing as a tool of research, on the other hand, was something quite foreign.

The sketchbooks I gave to my class became a mnemonic tool for recording the history of Texas and the cultural influences on building in local landscapes. Early settlers from Spain, Mexico, Germany, Poland, France, and America, among others places, were building structures that on the one hand were culturally reminiscent of their homelands and on the other were influenced by local culture and materials available in the rugged Texas landscape. Students recorded buildings of stone, brick, adobe, jacal, and straw and the tectonics of their various elements: the textures, the grain, the patterns, the connections they made, and the shadows they cast.

Important to the journey of their sketchbooks was not only the recording of these cultural building traditions, but the landscapes themselves. Pages were filled with the sweeping horizons, the dramatic mountains, the rocks, and various trees of the landscape. The students would pause at a site to draw a building, but also began to simply draw the landscape of that building, how it connected to the spirit of the place. They began to understand the 'belonging' by sitting, observing, and sketching.

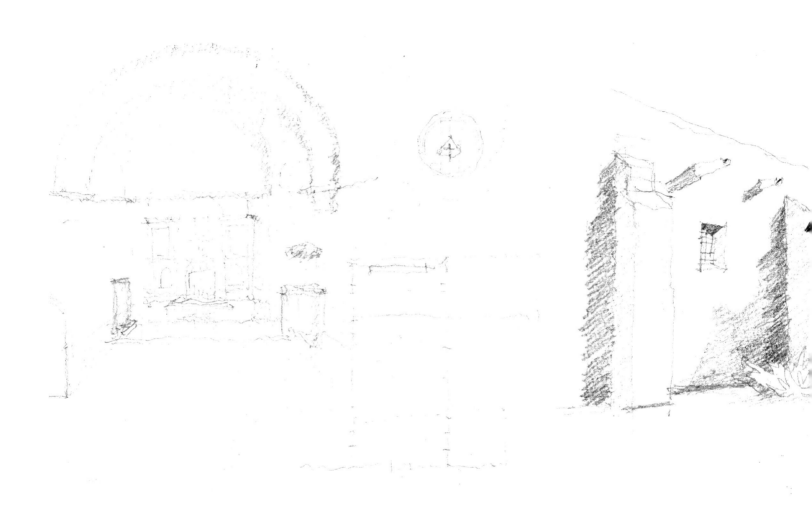

A record of the tectonics and forms that make these buildings
so impressive. The shadows show that the artist has carefully
understood the way the light would hit the building. Max Baum,
'22 Yale Student, *Mission Santo Espiritu, Gonzales, Texas*.
Graphite sketch.

MISSION SANTO
ESPIRITU

GOURD 02·13·2022

At the end of the journey, the students sketched their concepts for a cultural center—ideas that they would carry back to begin the design process in the studio. Their observations on site would continue to inform their designs in New Haven. They would sketch plans with an understanding of material and experience through a connection to the landscape and culture.

This process of representational design has been used for generations but is now quickly giving way to computer simulation. In the traditional process of drawing, observation forms ideas and stimulates the imagination. Imagination creates a concept to be teased out on paper, manipulated, layered, minute adjustment after minute adjustment. Sometimes accidental lines become part of the design, or a simple scribble carries the eye of a composition, form, or detail. These nuances are further congealed into aesthetic solutions that become the architect's vision of a building or structure.

Computers aid design in numerous ways and some talented individuals produce spectacular results on them. But the technology tends to bypass much of this process of assimilation. It removes the natural transformation from observation to solution. Whereas drawing, especially well-practiced drawing, allows an architect to fluidly and immediately express their ideas and thoughts on paper; the process of inputting for a computer's processing interrupts thought processes, and the programmed actions of software leads our solutions to what the machine or program often allows. A computer can never draw a rock in a way that there is an understanding of the rock—to be the rock, and to understand how the rock feels in our hand as it is used to build a wall. Solutions no longer allow for subtle, mental understandings of nature and what it offers us in terms of achieving beauty, or what it offers through our human interpretation. Our feelings, our moods, our cultural beliefs, and our relationship with the natural world and with each other as human beings—our humanity—is left out of the equation of design.

My Yale students seemed to be excited by the opportunity to sketch, which was unfamiliar to some of them. It was certainly unexpected to be drawing a landscape sans architecture. It gave them a sense of freedom and discovery. Not every student who sketches will be particularly proficient in the techniques required, particularly at the beginning. That could hardly be expected. But the object is not to produce a beautiful work of art, so much as to train the individual's powers of observation and provide a useful means of developing architectural ideas. It is the action of doing—the process of drawing—that encourages a certain understanding, and that understanding can lead one to solutions. Eye to pencil, pencil to paper, make a permanent connection between object and mind. I hope they will all find it useful in the pursuit of their chosen careers.

Once they were back in the studio, students used sketches from the trip to create a concept for an architectural compound. Max Baum, '22 Yale Student. Graphite sketch.

Students began to understand vernacular forms and how they could
be used to resolve contemporary problems. Drawings such as
these were exercises in being able to analyze architecture through a
sketchbook: older forms could be used to inspire modern designs.
Max Kronauer, '22 Yale Student, *A Study of Vernacular Forms*.
Graphite sketch.

Seeing through Drawing

"The greatest thing a human soul ever does in this world is to see something and to tell what it saw in a plain way. Hundreds of people can talk for one who can think, but thousands can think for one who can see. To see clearly is poetry, prophecy and religion, all in one."

John Ruskin, *Modern Painters*, 1894

Historically, if we wanted to know the nature of a place, a person, or a thing—to penetrate beneath surface appearance to reach a more profound understanding—we tried to look through the eyes of an artist. This was how artists saw the world. They analyzed it. And even if their aim was simply to achieve a representation of reality, they could not help interpreting it according to their own cultural filters or artistic points of view, whether this was a conscious process or not.

Ideas were born through writing or drawing. Scientists sketched hypotheses, explorers sketched places, and architects drew spaces, buildings and cities. At one time—think of Raphael and Michelangelo—architects actually were artists: they had to both observe and conceive through drawing and painting. This is how they understood space and dimension. This allowed their imaginations to flourish and conceive of an architecture that had never been realized before. Even in quite recent times, some architects actually started as artists—painters, observing nature first. These were empirical learners.

It seemed that architects were given an almost divine gift: to conjure a thing in their mind and to transmute that idea, through their art, into the realm of three-dimensional reality, into physical being. Almost as importantly, architects used their artistic gifts to observe the world and to understand it, for only then could they seek to reinterpret it. Through these interpretive abilities they would also explore the reasons for being.

Ruskin made the connection between painting and architecture, believing that anyone could learn to draw if they dedicated enough time to it. He was among the first to put forward a process for learning how to create fine drawings. John Ruskin (1819-1900), *Tower of the Cathedral at Sens*, c. 1845. Pen and brown ink, brush and black ink, black chalk, and watercolor over graphite on brown paper, 16″ x 12 ¹/₁₆″.

This ability to understand and to conceive complex forms and put them on paper separated architects from builders. Drawing was the architect's craft.

Today, many art schools no longer require drawing, even as a skill for admission to the profession, and in turn, most architectural programs have stopped requiring architects to draw by hand, since knowing how to draw by hand is not necessary to operate a computer and describe form and space. But what about the other part of the process— the observing? What about seeing? What about the development of the creative mind, and the imagination of an architect?

Architects today remain intensely visual. Simulation and visual graphics play a major role in how they conceive ideas and communicate them. And as they travel, they take thousands of photographs of buildings and their environments. Yet these images are what I'd consider a 'capture' as opposed to a 'response'. A response connects to our own experiences, memories and recall. A mere capture fails to empirically connect to the graphic solutions we produce in our digital world.

I've always considered drawing as something of another language; the more you draw, the more fluent you become at translating what is in your 'mind's eye'. In fact, if you are truly fluent, there is no 'translation.' Just as with your mother tongue, you say exactly and directly what you are thinking. In other words, the person who is fluent in drawing can lay out the object in their mind without the hindrance of a 'translation filter:' the thought directly flows from mind to paper, and thus to matter. Descartes expressed a profound philosophical truth in his phrase, 'I am thinking therefore I exist.' An architect could say, 'I draw, therefore I am.'

Above: Ruskin believed that to draw the leaf was to understand the forest: close attention to detail illuminated the larger scene. John Ruskin (1819-1900), *Rocks and Ferns in a Wood at Crossmount, Perthshire,* 1847. Pen and ink, watercolor and bodycolor on paper, 12 ¹¹/₁₆" x 18 ⁵/₁₆".

Left: Natural forms were all important to Ruskin who drew them with minute attention to their structure. John Ruskin (1819-1900), "The Acanthus of Torcello" in *John Ruskin: The Stones of Venice,* 1898.

Similarly, when architects sketch places they want to study or remember, the hand helps to channel their observations to the memory of their minds. This is not simply a visual matter, but a kind of synesthesia, or cross-sensory recording. All the senses take part. As you paint the field, you smell the grass, hear the birds and the crickets singing, you feel the wind in your hair and the sun on your back. As your draw or paint, you fix that place in your mind through the senses by which you experience it.

As an architect, drawing and painting are at the center of who I am and what I do. I must paint in order to see and I must draw in order to convey thought. It is how I understand shape, form, color, composition, scale, shadow and light, and it is how I describe it to the world.

Language and drawing were among the earliest forms of communication. Yet many drop drawing as they adapt to other forms of communication, while some continue to use it as an important way to express ideas. We continue to draw as a way of expression through our lives. Imagine a world where all language was digitally simulated by artificial intelligence. Would that mean we would lose what it means to be human? Expression is key to our humanity, whether through language or—for architects down the centuries—through drawing. It creates social interaction and carries symbolic meaning. It understands the 'why' in what we do and how we see things.

It seems to me that computers have their own language. And just as computers speak a different language to ordinary discourse, and reading on a screen is different from studying hard copy or reading a book, so computer drawing techniques are not the same as pencil on paper. It is said that books allow us to read between the lines, to insert ourselves in the narrative, to become a part of it. With simulation the story is set, whereas—I would suggest—drawing generally allows more spontaneity. For the moment at least, thought moves more fluently from mind to paper than it does to the screen. As technology becomes ever more sophisticated this could change, but, as things are at present, the computer, however skillful the person manipulating it may be, does not fully replicate the act of drawing.

For centuries drawing has been the medium through which we connect and express our imagination, and as architects that has been central to who we are as a profession. It is our craft. The act of drawing is part of the creative process. Through it we discover how ideas relate to nature and material, space, and light. We formulate, we rearrange, we learn. We can return to a singular landscape and see something new, something different, time and time again, how it changes in every moment in response to a season, to a particular light, to a particular moment and through our own current experiences, emotions, and moods. We see it how we wish to see it. We shape it to our own perceptions; to our ideas of composition, color, and relationships of the parts to the whole; and to the landscape's relationship to us and our culture. In other words, drawing helps us to understand the surrounding world and in turn, shape it.

Richardson's pencil flows across the page to create order and rhythm. Often simple incidental marks on a page would later become incorporated into the building's design. Henry Hobson Richardson (1838-1886), *Perspective, preliminary drawing. Chicago, Ill. Marshall Field Wholesale Store (MF)*, 1885-1887. Graphite and watercolor on Manila paper, 11 $^{13}/_{16}$" x 20 $^{1}/_{16}$".

An American Tradition

"I am nature."

Jackson Pollock

Jackson Pollock spoke those words at a time when the idea of art was changing. Previously, art had provided a cultural representation of the outside world. As suggested by Bowdoin College Museum of Art's exhibit, "This Is a Portrait If I Say So" (referencing American artist, Robert Rauschenberg's note to a Paris dealer in 1961), once photography became a primary tool for representation with "irrefutable likeness", the artist turned to their own personal conception of representation and could feel free to paint that which cannot be seen. Now that art rejected literal representation, it increasingly became self-referential; the artist's internal processes were what mattered, the subject matter was his or her own mind. The art of painting did not necessarily seek to portray anything at all but could now be an end in itself. While artists like Pollock and Wyeth sat side by side in New York's Museum of Modern Art, Pollock was seen as achieving grand heights of artistic achievement, where a representational artist like his contemporary Andrew Wyeth was considered sentimental. In other words, the art world valued self-expression over cultural expression. Popular culture was no longer the arbiter of meaning—the artist was.

Architecture has followed the same path. The profession holds that popular culture should not dictate taste, because only the architect is now the deliverer of that truth. To believe otherwise is said to be sentimental or nostalgic.

Before the 20th century, art had always been closely aligned with our cultural beliefs. Art followed those beliefs and continuously expressed them, often with reference to, and reverence for, the work of the past. This created a palimpsest of cultural thought and symbolism of meaning within its many layers. Today, contemporary sales far outstrip other categories in the auction houses. This turns its back on the observation of the natural world, which was a strong American tradition until the mid-1900s.

A reflection of the idea that nature is God's refuge for the poet-hero: close observation leads to an understanding of God and Truth. Thomas Moran (1837-1926), *Man Under the Trees*, 1865. 8 13/16″ x 10 3/16″.

In the 19th century, representations of the dramatic American landscape formed the backdrop to the national story. It was through paintings that the general public began to find their identity as Americans. As a young nation, America sought to distinguish its identity separate from the established aristocratic institutions of Europe. In Boston, preacher Ralph Waldo Emerson saw the universe as two equal components: nature and soul. In this he was profoundly influenced by the Swiss theologian Emmanuel Swedenborg, who believed that there was a direct relationship between the spirit and nature. Emerson's short book, *Nature*, published in 1836 would become the most read book in 19th-century America and would change the course of American art for the next one hundred years. In the introduction, Emerson declares that, "There are new lands, new men, new thoughts [in this new nation]." At a time when American artists were in Florence painting European themes in European landscapes, Emerson called for an American art; one which would be shaped by the landscape and reflect the ideals of a new nation's future in art, poetry, literature, and politics. Nature was the language of man—how we thought and how we talked. "Every appearance in nature corresponds to some state of the mind." Emerson would push Americans away from literal interpretation of the Bible, towards secularism and science.

For the first time in American art we begin to see metaphors represented in our landscapes: metaphors that represent our vision for the future of our country, our relationship with God, our spirituality, our unbound bounty of resources, and our perceived right as a nation to forge a living from a wilderness.

Emerson's writings would usher art in America onto the world stage through American Luminism and the Transcendentalist Movement. New England artists such as Fitz Henry Lane and Emerson's friend, John Frederick Kensett saw the ethereal light captured by J.M.W. Turner in his epic canvases and developed similar techniques to paint purely American scenes. Lane left Boston to cruise the shores of Maine and paint the other-worldly radiance of the shoulder times of the day, dawn and sunset. They spoke of the divinity that pervades nature and touches humankind. Sunrise evoked the dawn of our country as a nation.

Around the same period the Hudson River School attempted to express the ideal relationship between man and an all-powerful nature. They believed that by seeing, one would know truth and know God. Thomas Cole's landscapes were an expression of the delicate balance between humanity and all-powerful nature, whilst John Frederick Kensett's calm meditative landscapes were illuminated by God's glow of ethereal light. In the work of Thomas Moran, man was the poet-hero; the human beings who appear in his awe-inspiring American landscapes seem to be in the presence of God.

Meanwhile, the big cities were on the move. People from New York and Boston were adventuring into the wilderness for leisure purposes, romanticizing the virgin landscape as a God-given paradise uncorrupted by industry. The dramatic paintings of the West were unveiled at sensational events, where room size paintings were undraped in front of

Right (top): Influenced by Turner and the Luminist Movement, Lane depicts the trinity between sky, land, and water as well as the importance of man's reflection. Fitz Henry Lane (1804-1865), *Brace's Rock, Brace's Cove*, 1864. Oil on canvas, 10 ¼" x 15 ¼".

Right (bottom): Kensett was an early member of the Hudson River School. His paintings displayed the ethereal quality of Emerson's *Nature* and of the Transcendentalism Movement. The image is remarkable for its indelible sense of calm, clarity, and quiet, exemplary of his contemplative style. John Frederick Kensett (1816-1872), *Beacon Rock, Newport Harbor*, 1857. Oil on canvas, 22 ½" x 36".

an awe-inspired crowd. This was the age of American expansionism. The 19th-century doctrine of Manifest Destiny proclaimed what was then perceived as our nation's God-given right to expand into and control the landscapes of the West. Yet painting these landscapes helped to crystallize the desire to preserve the wild natural beauty of Yosemite and elsewhere, and led to the creation of the world's first national park system.

This American Romanticism was shattered by the Civil War. The nation was torn apart and disunited. Artists became illustrators of a conflict, reporting back home the horrors of war. From the war there emerged a new breed of artists. Ones like Winslow Homer painted idealistic paintings of bucolic brotherhood: a society rejoined, or perhaps one should say partially rejoined, since he often portrayed the black population as on the outside, seeking a place in the new order. Homer still found inspiration in the landscape, especially where the land met the sea. "Painting was not the answer," writes Donald Goddard, "but the constant and obsessive search."

Above: A depiction of the ideal relationship between humanity and all-powerful nature. Note how inconsequential the figures are with regards to the power of nature. Thomas Cole (1801-1848), *Distant View of Niagara Falls*, 1830. Oil on panel, 18 7/8" x 23 7/8".

As the nation recovered and prosperity returned, Aestheticism sought to relieve art from the burden of its moral purpose. Art was for art's sake, beauty its purpose, and nature forever central. In London, John Ruskin rose to prominence as a Victorian sage, writing voluminously on art and architecture before championing social reform. In *The Elements of Drawing*, Ruskin claimed that anyone could learn to draw if they took simple steps to learning and put in the numerous hours of practice needed. "For his system he claimed only that it was calculated to encourage refinement of individual perception, to train the eye in close observation of natural beauties and the hand in delicacy and precision of manipulation," notes Lawrence Campbell. Keenness of observation was at the heart of it. Ruskin's teaching on the visual separation of colors is said is said to have launched the Impressionist movement in France.

Yet Ruskin believed that in the greatest art, observation had to be augmented by imagination—it was what separated Fine Art from mere art. As he wrote in *The Elements of Drawing*: "For it is the imagination, unrestrained by scientific knowledge and preconceived ideas, which enables the artist to travel beyond appearances." In *Modern Painters*, Ruskin expressed a similar idea in a fanciful image:

> *We do not want [the artist's] mind to be as badly blown glass, that distorts what we see through it; but like a glass of sweet and strange color, that gives new tones to what we see through it; and a glass of rare strength and clearness too, to let us see more than we could ourselves.*

Right: For Homer, painting was about the constant, obsessive search to understand nature. Winslow Homer (1836-1910), *Glass Windows, Bahamas*, ca. 1885. Watercolor and graphite on paper, 13 15/16" x 20 1/16".

Inspired by William Morris and the Arts and Crafts Movement, artists, craftsmen, and architects of the late 19th century turned away from materialism. Beauty was all. Artists such as John LaFarge worked alongside architects like William Morris Hunt to incorporate decorative schemes of nature into his architecture. LaFarge's traveling companion, John Singer Sargent, rose to international prominence, first as a painter of high-society portraits, then as a watercolorist whose distinctive bravado brush strokes captured "moments in time", generally in his scenes painted abroad. Sargent's ability to capture the essence of light and movement was his signature.

Once again, war disrupted art's dance with culture. Social views changed after the First World War, as well as the way artists came to express both our natural and cultural landscapes. Socially conscious Modern Regionalists of the New York School began to express landscapes, and our cultural relationships with those landscapes, differently. George Bellows and N.C. Wyeth, father of Andrew Wyeth and grandfather to Jamie Wyeth, began to portray the interactions of working men with the landscapes from which they had scraped a living for generations. The dynamic backdrop of the Maine Coast, in places like Port Clyde and Monhegan, set the perfect stage for expressing the daily toil of a fisherman within an iconic American landscape. Edward Hopper and Rockwell Kent were among those who joined the community on Monhegan. Here, they found their voice as artists as they painted emotions, time and place into their coastal landscapes. It was what John Ruskin called, "Measuring the moods of nature."

Edward Hopper, "the Poet of Silence," began to see the landscape as blocks of color and it was here that he began to develop what art critic Walter Wells called a synesthesia, or cross sensory imagery: "Artists have the ability to have us taste what we see, or hear what we feel, to give odorful color, melodious flavor, or a chill wind perceived as a wailing siren or a quivering blue light." It was on this rugged working island of Monhegan that Rockwell Kent said, "I want to paint the rhythm of eternity."

Maine continues to be a haven for American artists. American Realist Bo Bartlett continues to paint in the tradition of Edward Hopper, and the Wyeth family legacy continues with Jamie Wyeth painting the landscapes of Mid-Coast Maine.

Wyeth, like Ruskin, measured the moods of nature. N.C. Wyeth (1882-1945), *Black Spruce Ledge (Lobstering Off Black Spruce Ledge)*. Tempera on hardboard, 33 ½" x 42".

Dramatic, awe-inspiring scenes of nature such as these attracted
a paying public in the 19th century. Hidden behind curtains, they
would be unveiled in a theatrical display of America, a vast nation
shaped by brotherhood, humanity, and ecology. Albert Bierstadt
(1830-1902), *Among the Sierra Nevada, California*. Oil on canvas,
72" x 120 ⅛".

Paintings like this helped to make the great landscapes and
wilderness part of the national identity of America. Yellowstone was
made the first National Park soon after Moran's painting. Thomas
Moran (1837-1926), *The Grand Canyon of the Yellowstone*, 1872.
Oil on canvas, mounted on aluminum, 84" x 144 ¼".

Church's painting of Niagra Falls was indicative of the inspiring
paintings of the American landscape, made more dramatic by being
presented on an epic-sized canvas. Frederic Edwin Church (1826-
1900), *Niagara*, 1857. Oil on canvas, 40" x 90 ½".

Gifford was an ardent painter of nature and landscapes. He found many influences in other painters, but avoided affiliation with artist groups or schools in case it displaced the inspiration he found directly from being in nature. Sanford Robinson Gifford (1823-1880), *The Artist Sketching at Mount Desert, Maine*, 1864-1865. Oil on canvas, 11″ x 19″.

Hopper's paintings have the quality of a phenomenon known as synesthesia or cross-sensory imagery which heightened the emotional charge of his portrayals of loneliness and silence. As Walter Wells described it in *Silent Theatre: The Art of Edward Hopper*: "Artists … have the power to cross and tangle our senses with imagery that makes us taste what we see, hear what we feel, give us odorful color, melodious flavor, or a chill wind perceived as a wailing siren or a quavering blue light." Edward Hopper (1882-1967), *Corn Hill (Truro, Cape Cod)*, 1930. Oil on canvas, 28 ½" x 42 ½".

Bogdanove studied architecture at Columbia University and trained
under Francis Davis Millet, the country's leading muralist. He would
summer on Monhegan Island, Maine, where he painted alongside
the likes of George Bellows, Rockwell Kent, and Edward Hopper.
Abraham Bogdanove (1887-1946), *Whitehead from Gull Rock*.
39 ¾″ x 35 ½″.

Hopper, a member of the Monhegan Island Art Colony, saw the landscape not as a collection of objects, but as a series of abstract blocks of color. Edward Hopper (1882-1967), *Rocks and Sea*, 1916-1919. Oil on wood, 11 ¾" x 16 1/16".

An example of Homer's observations of the interactions between land and sea. Winslow Homer (1836-1910), *Northeaster*. Oil on canvas, 34 1/2″ x 50″.

Kent described the scene: "The windblown ocean plain stretched dark as indigo to a horizon knife-sharp against the golden lower sky; from gold became the imperceptible gradations of emerald, and the emerald became cobalt; and the cobalt, a deep purple at the Zenith—often so dark, that Zenith sky, that one could see the moon by day and almost, one imagined the stars." Rockwell Kent (1882-1971), *Calm and Free (Maine Coast)*. Oil on canvas, 28 3/8" x 44 1/8".

The Artist's Hand

"One is not a good architect unless he is an artist. Otherwise, he is just a mechanic."

George Bellows, *American Architect*, 1920

I left Texas for New England to pursue a knowledge of traditional architecture that I couldn't get at home. I was looking for a broader understanding of traditional design and of the architects of the past who served as heroes in their built and illustrated work. I was instinctively drawn to those who sketched, and discovered that together they formed a robust American tradition on both the East and West Coasts.

Discovering architects like Bertram Goodhue changed how I looked at architectural drawings. These weren't just renderings, these were art; they carried the eye to what the architect needed you to see, a shadow over a steeple or a sweeping lawn leading you eye to a particular element, a heavy line lending importance to a detail. Composition played a large role in these drawings, leading the eye around the drawing, never resting but pausing at important moments. These moments carried through to his final designs: design emerged from the process of drawing, and the composition of a building followed the composition of the drawing. Form and detail followed the rules of beauty established by seeing as an artist.

Goodhue started his career as a gifted illustrator in New York, but knowing he wanted to pursue architecture as a profession he went to Boston. As a young architect in Boston, Goodhue was a member of a group of young artistic intellectuals that formed The Society of Arts and Crafts in 1897. He soon boarded a train for El Paso, Texas, from where he took Mexican burros across the Rio Grande. Mexico was a visual feast that would form the basis for his book *Mexican Memories: The Record of a Slight Sojourn below the Yellow Rio Grande.*

A travel sketch by Abele, the first black American to graduate as an architect from the University of Pennsylvania. Julian Francis Abele (1881-1950), *Church from Plaza*. Watercolor on woven paper, not signed.

Goodhue delighted in Mexican culture and sketched his observations of both the Spanish Colonial architecture as well as the Mexican senoritas he surrounded himself with. These observations served him well. The design of the 1915 Pan American Exhibition in San Diego was expected to go to local architect Irving Gill, but Goodhue, with a vision inspired by his explorations of Mexico, won the commission as lead architect, designing the most significant project in America to date shaped by regional cultural roots and influences. This brought American architecture to an understanding of local place and culture.

Boston architects placed a unique focus on drawing, not just in the sense of drafting, but as a means to understand the world in which they were building through their eyes. This was a period that gave rise to the architect-artist. Journals such as that of the Boston Architectural Club published their members' travel drawings and studies of landscape. The role of drawing grew beyond merely that of being a tool of architecture; to be a good architect, it was thought, one must be a good artist. Luminaries of the Boston architectural scene such as H.H. Richardson, William R. Emerson, and Robert Peabody of Peabody & Stearns sought to connect their architecture to the landscape through art.

The dramatic Maine Coast caught the imagination of these architects as their landed Victorian clients began building on the craggy shores where the land met the sea. It was a primal American landscape that captured America's character as well as its nautical culture. Architects often drew and painted together as colleagues, setting aside any competitiveness for their love of nature and the landscapes in which they were building. Robert Peabody was a particular figurehead as he mentored and taught other architects to draw from nature to inspire their work.

John Calvin Stevens maintained a friendship with the Boston architect William R. Emerson, who would become the first dean of architecture at MIT. Stevens had been born in the city but his parents moved to Maine when he was two. Staying in the state, he ran a thriving architectural office from Portland, Maine, whose style was described as displaying a "primitive simplicity and wholesome vigor". Stevens' work started with the knowledge of the sites on which he built. His almost ceremonial review of the landscapes in which he built, he called the "Seeing of the Site". This view of the importance of the landscape extended to his painting. Stevens was central to the landscape painting scene of Maine. He designed the clubhouse for the Portland Society of Art, of which he was a dedicated member. He invited architects to join him on bicycle sketching tours of Normandy and would enthusiastically ask fellow architects, "Do you sketch?" Letting his colleagues know they will have "no shortage of opportunity to improve our skills." In Maine he formed a painting club called the "Brush'uns", with whom he painted landscapes and had many art exhibits. He drew often with Emerson and Peabody and became a respected artist in his own right, drawing inspiration from the landscape through his art. His architecture embraced modern living for the middle class—a middle class seeking a relationship with nature. In France the Impressionists

Peabody, of the Boston firm Peabody & Stearns, believed strongly in the importance for an architect of drawing, and filled his sketchbook with scenes of the coast. Robert Swain Peabody (1845-1917), *Newport, Rhode Island*.

were introducing their middle-class collectors to a new way of viewing landscape; according to the art historian Vincent Scully, the work of Stevens and his friends was an American parallel and launched what would become the shingle style—America's first truly indigenous style of architecture and considered by many prescient of modern design in America.

When Winslow Homer was looking for an architect to build on the Maine Coast, Stevens was a natural choice. He designed both Homer's studio The Ark, in Prout's

Neck, and later his home known as the Kettle Cove. After the job was finished, Stevens' invoice asked for any painting by Winslow Homer. In return, he received a note from the artist:

> *I am very much surprised & pleased at your bill. This kind of thing occurs seldom in matters of business. The interest you have shown in this cottage of mine & the valuable time you have given to it in your busy season & your success in producing it, shows me that I can greet you as a brother artist & thanking you sincerely, I send you this sketch of mine that I think is appropriate & will please you.*

Stevens not only received a painting of the artist's studio in the fog, but a friendship and generous mentoring from Homer in his painting of landscapes.

As in the Renaissance era, some American architects started as artists. The first monograph on an American architect was on the work of Charles Platt and was considered the bible of modern American design when it came out in 1913. He had barely three years earlier changed his official profession in the business directory from "artist" to "architect", and he was said to have entered architecture "through the garden gate".

Platt was born in New York City and as a boy gained a reputation for his atmospheric etchings, an art recently revived in the Boston area. However it was in France that he grew to have a love of landscape, ancient places, and painting. He spent much of his early life in Paris where he studied art at the Académie Julian. Here, he favored the Dutch School of art over his colleagues' interest in the Barbizon school. When Platt returned to the States, he followed one of his mentors, Stephen Parrish, to New Hampshire where he joined in painting landscapes with the Cornish Art Colony together with

artists such as Augustus Saint-Gaudens, Daniel Chester French, and Steven Parrish's son, Maxfield Parrish. Through these landscapes he showed a clear tendency towards Aestheticism.

Platt and his brother, William, worked for Frederick Law Olmstead, and Charles, fearing young William was not receiving a proper education in the art of landscape design, took his brother to Rome in 1892 to do measured drawings of the gardens of the villas of the Renaissance. Returning, Charles published several richly-illustrated articles on Italian gardens, soon expanding to become the first illustrated book in English on the subject and the most important on the formal Italian gardens in America. He quickly became known as America's foremost landscape architect in the emerging revival of the Formal American garden. Soon Charles was enlisting his young friend, Stanford White, as his draftsman. His blending of the casual lifestyle of New England with the formality of Rome brought him almost overnight success as one of America's pre-eminent architects of the American Renaissance.

The New England tradition had a parallel on the West Coast, where California was among the first states to find its identity through the Arts and Crafts Movement. The environmentalist John Muir, and novelist Jack London began to expound a cultural view of California's dramatic wilderness landscapes. This was a time when architects such as A.C. Schweinfurth, Ernest Coxhead, John Galen Howard and Benard Maybeck began roaming the countryside sketching early cultural influences of Spain in Californian vernacular architecture. Landscape and culture merged with architecture to produce a new entity.

Left: Goodhue's sketchbook of Mexico heavily influenced his ideas on the architecture of Regionalism, as first expressed at Balboa Park during the Pan American Exposition of 1915 in San Diego. Bertram G. Goodhue (1869-1924), *Cabrillo Bridge*, 1914. 4" x 5".

Right: A depiction of Homer's studio on Prout's Neck in the fog. If not the actual painting given to Stevens in return for architectural work, it is one very similar. Winslow Homer (1836-1910), *The Artist's Studio in an Afternoon Fog*, 1894. Oil on canvas, 24" x 30 ¼".

Although nowadays best known for his prominence in the world
of architecture, Platt started his career as an artist. He painted this
scene of Normandy while on his way to study at the Académie Julian
in Paris. Charles Adam Platt (1861-1933), *Low Tide Sussex*.

Platt developed the first measured drawings of Italian Gardens
and went on to work for Frederick Law Olmstead. Charles Adam
Platt (1861-1933), *Hartford, Connecticut*, 1885. Oil on panel,
10 ½" x 13 ¾".

The success of the great Beaux-Arts practice of McKim, Mead & White spawned other firms. Willis Polk left their office in New York to head West, joining a young man from England, Ernest Coxhead, first in Los Angeles and then on the the Bay Area. Coxhead brought with him the teachings of John Ruskin and William Morris. Their arrival in California coincided with the sensation of Jack London's book *The Call of the Wild*. The author had been a tenant at a simple, "beautifully situated" house in Piedmont on the North Bay built in 1878 by Boston preacher Joseph Worcester. Worcester was educated at Harvard Scientific School and was heavily influenced by the writings of Ruskin, Emerson, and Wordsworth. He was also aligned with his friend John Muir's beliefs in nature. Muir saw the Yosemite Valley, where he built his house with a stream running under his bed and was said to be sustained by reading Emerson, as God's church. Muir would later go on to be the co-founder of the Sierra Club, and would be forever known as the father of environmentalism.

Worcester's house was much more conventional but attuned to nature all the same. Low-slung rooflines and redwood clapboards were left to weather, much like the simple shingle structures back home in New England, reflecting his teachings that man should be closely aligned with nature, and therefore to God. This simple house in the Piedmont Hills would become an inspiration for a new generation of Bay Area architects and Worcester their prophet. The design of his Swedenborgian Church in Pacific Heights would go further.

Polk and Coxhead, and a small group including Bernard Maybeck, followed Worcester's teachings on nature closely and began to build a community of young architects and artists around the principles of simple buildings connected to the landscape, craft, and culture. Willis Polk's *Architectural Journal* galvanized this movement of building in harmony with the landscape. Their first buildings were very much influenced by those the Bostonians were designing in Maine.

Educated at MIT, Howard often travelled California's coastline with other Bay Area architects sketching the Spanish architecture of the area. He would later lead U.C. Berkley's architecture program, advocating an architecture that was in tune with nature. John Galen Howard (1864-1931), *Sketch of a house in southern California*, 1888. 10" x 14".

Worcester served as advisor to this architectural community, and when he decided to build his church he called on A. Page Brown to whom Maybeck was apprenticed. The Swedenborgian Church in Pacific Heights was, in its every detail, to bring its occupants closer to nature. It was similar to the work of the English Arts and Crafts architects, C.F.A. Voysey and Baillie Scott, and of the Bostonians whom we have already met where the collaboration of H.H Richardson, LaFarge and Augustus Saint-Gaudens in Boston's Trinity Church was a model of total comprehensive design. Yet, unlike these counterparts who detailed and highly decorated the interiors of their houses, the church was to remain raw and natural with its structural members, exposed timbers carted from the Muir Woods, expressed in the vernacular way and decorated with the boughs of trees and clumps—a greenery gathered from nature. Upon entering the church, the intimate and warm effect was immediately felt.

This Church would serve as inspiration for the next generation of young architects like Julia Morgan, A.C. Schweinfurth, John Galen Howard, and Daniel Burnham, as well as transformative for Page's young draftsman, Bernard Maybeck. Born in New York City, Maybeck was educated in Paris at the École des Beaux-Arts and after working for the New York office of Carrère and Hastings arrived in the Bay area where he became yet another tenant of Worcester's Piedmont house. Maybeck's interest in the relationship of architecture to the landscape had been nurtured in the Beaux-Arts atelier of the landscape architect Louis-Jules André. It could be said that Maybeck's principles of architecture's sensitivity to the landscape were to become one of the underlying principles of the Bay Region's architecture.

Howard, who came to the West Coast from MIT and had worked in the offices of McKim, Mead & White, and H.H. Richardson eventually helped move the Bay Area movement away from historicism and towards "a spirit of simplicity" driven by the landscape and the simple materials it had to offer. Howard would go on to be the first Dean of Berkley's School of Architecture.

Other California architects found their voice through art and their interpretation of its landscape. After Bertram Goodhue shone a light on Southern California's Spanish heritage, artist George Washington Smith built his own studio in Montecito in the Spanish Andulsian style, and took advantage of Southern California's mild Mediterranean climate to transplant the complete Spanish scene of agave, succulents, and cacti. Smith had studied art at the University of Pennsylvania and architecture at Harvard, but unable to graduate he tried his hand at bond trading where he made a fortune, allowing him to follow his dream of art and painting in Europe where he ended up attending the Académie Julian in Paris. Following the outbreak of war in 1914, Washington returned to the States where he exhibited his art with George Bellows. Exhibiting at the Pan American Exhibition in San Diego in 1915, he found Southern California to his liking and settled in Santa Barbara.

Left: Morgan, later one of California's most celebrated architects, studied under John Galen Howard at U.C. Berkley and was the first woman admitted to the École des Beaux-Arts in Paris. Julia Morgan (1872-1957), *Late medieval-era hill town with towers*, c. 1900. Graphite and watercolor, 4 1/2" x 8 9/16".

Above: Pries's Art Deco design for the rebuilding of Santa Barbara after the 1925 earthquake. The Bothin Building was one of the structures that shaped what is today Santa Barbara's romantic aesthetic. Lionel H. Pries (1897-1968), *Preliminary scheme of Bothin Building, Santa Barbara, California*, 1925. Watercolor, 8 1/2" x 14 1/2".

The little studio that Smith built for himself was an instant hit with the landed Californians. It launched him into a lifelong career that would define Southern California regionalism, created some of Santa Barbara's most iconic structures, and redefined the city as one in tune with its landscape and cultural heritage. Interestingly, Smith did not do the renderings that defined his artistic work as an architect; his style was defined by the hand of his young draftswoman, Lutah Maria Riggs. Riggs's artful renderings became synonymous with Washington's work. Riggs continued to work until 1980, half a century after Washington's death in 1930, becoming California's first woman Fellow in the American Institute of Architects.

Architect and educator Lionel Pries was one of the last great architects of the tradition. Dedicated to educating young architects at the University of Washington from 1928 until 1958, his story was one of great inspiration and creativity. His development as an educator and as an architect was informed by his deep understanding of landscape through his paintings. His own education was shaped by his travels through Europe which he recorded enthusiastically in painting.

Born in San Francisco, Pries was greatly influenced by the city's deep architectural roots in Arts and Crafts and the role of nature, craft, and art in architecture and design. He followed Ernest Coxhead, Bernard Maybeck and others in their development of a California aesthetic based upon these principles. Following Bertram Goodhue's regional Spanish references at Balboa Park in 1915, his work in the early 1920s greatly impacted the aesthetic fabric of Santa Barbara's reconstruction following the earthquake of 1925.

As an architect and educator, Pries's art played a major role. His work closely followed the art of the Modern Ruralists, especially those of the West like Georgia O'Keefe and Marsden Hartley. His landscape paintings from Mexico and the Northwest show a fluidity in line that he carried into his architecture, and the colors found in his landscapes gave a vibrant life to his buildings. Pries's own perspective on art was so respected that he was appointed director of what was to later become The Art Institute of Seattle.

But by the end of Pries's career the drawing techniques used by his generation had come to seem antiquated. I discovered this for myself when, as a young man, I left the East Coast and returned to Texas in order once again to explore the local cultural roots that had taken my interest in my youth. Joining an office in San Antonio, I met John Kell, the elderly father of one of the partners. He was originally from Boston. Already in his eighties, he sat quietly in the back ruminating over shop drawings. In the print room was a drawing, a huge Beaux-Arts watercolor framed on the wall—a tower over a seaside bastion, six feet long, beautifully and artistically painted. It was the only relic of John's past to be seen. He never spoke of his formative years as a young architect. Those memories had faded with the steady march of the Modern Movement, and as he saw it, a relic from the past.

John had come to San Antonio as a young architect to oversee the construction of the San Antonio Federal Courthouse in the early 1930s, as an associate under the auspices of Paul Cret. When the courthouse was finished he had stayed, his heart having been stolen by a Texas girl. John Kell was the first architect I had personally met from the generation of architect-artists. As a young student at the University of Pennsylvania, his artistic ability was considered at the top among his peers in an architectural program that still valued the Boston School of learning from drawing. His skills of drawing won him the prestigious Henry Gillette Woodman Traveling Scholarship, allowing him to travel to Europe to record the architecture that would influence his career. Upon returning and graduating from school, he took a desk at Paul Cret's office alongside fellow classmate, Louis Kahn. Here in San Antonio, he sat in the back of the studio, his artistic knowledge set aside, for time and the profession had moved on to looking at building through a more technical lens. Yet now I had been hired to sit at the front of the office, pencil and watercolors in hand, to carry forward a new vision of design for the firm.

By University of Pennsylvania student, John Kell, during his Henry Gillette Woodman Traveling Scholarship to Europe in 1931-1932. John Kell Sr. (1903-2002), *Ponte Pietra*, Verona, Italy. Watercolor, 10 ¾" x 14".

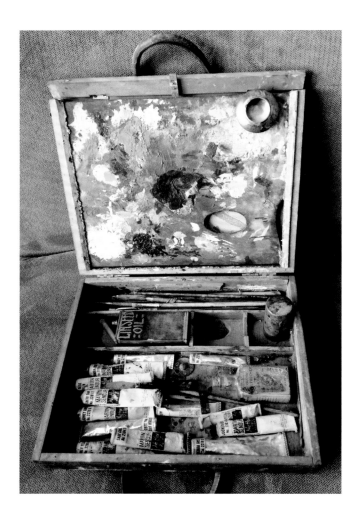

Stevens stated that he painted landscapes, not for the sake of art,
but as it was the only way to "see the site." John Calvin Stevens
(1855-1940), *John Calvin Stevens' Painting Kit*. Photograph.

Stevens' painting of Diamond Island off the coast of Maine illustrates
his search for understanding the landscapes in which he built. John
Calvin Stevens (1855-1940), *House Island from Little Diamond Island*.
Watercolor on paper, 9" x 13".

This fortified bridge was built during the Hundred Years War
between France and England. Begun in 1306, it was opened for
traffic in 1350 though not completed for another 38 years. Kell
chose a vantage point that makes the leading tower seem like a
heroic survival from the ancient past. John Kell Sr. (1903-2002),
Ponte Valentré, Cahors, France. Pencil and pastel, 13 ³/₄″ x 16 ³/₄″.
Completed during his Henry Gillette Woodman Traveling
Scholarship to Europe, 1931-32.

This medieval belltower in the Perpendicular style is a testament to Chipping Campden's wealth during the medieval period, when it was a center of the wool trade. At the turn of the 20th century, it became a focus of Arts and Crafts activity, and was later defended against inappropriate development by the etcher F. L. Griggs. Kell shows the scene under snow. John Kell Sr. (1903-2002), *Church of St. James*, Chipping Campden, England. Pencil and watercolor, 7 1/4" x 10". Completed during his Henry Gillette Woodman Traveling Scholarship to Europe, 1931-32.

To Boston architects like Peabody, sketching provided a tool for recording and analyzing architecture and its environment. (Facing page) This probably shows one of Peabody's own houses in relationship to its site. (This page) Watercolor provided the ideal medium to capture the texture of the old buildings that he saw on his European travels. Robert Swain Peabody (1845-1917), *Robert Swain Peabody Scrapbook*.

Travel sketch by Brunner, who was a student at MIT. Later, he was appointed to the U.S. Fine Arts Commission by Theodore Roosevelt and became an important city planner, developing plans for cities like Baltimore, Denver, Cleveland, and Albany New York. Caudebec-en-Caux is a town on the Seine estuary in Normandy, France. Arnold William Brunner (1857-1925), *Caudebec*. Graphite and white heightening on light blue-brown paper, 9 3/16″ x 5 11/16″.

This design of a rural chapel somewhere on the East Coast shows the influence of Peabody's travels abroad. Sketching helped him to understand and internalize the historic buildings that he saw in Europe, enabling him to incorporate ideas from them into his own work. Robert Swain Peabody (1845-1917), *Robert Swain Peabody Scrapbook*.

Above: Chamberlain would travel all over Europe doing etchings like this. Once again, observation is transmuted into architecture, illuminating the possibilities of built form. Samuel V. Chamberlain (1895-1975), *Harborside, Friendship, Maine*. Drypoint on paper, 8 1/2" x 12 3/4".

Right: Through his teaching at MIT's school of architecture, Chamberlain had a major influence on the painting and drawing of architecture on the East Coast. Samuel V. Chamberlain (1895–1975), American, *The Sunlit Tower, Colmar*. Etching and drypoint, 14 1/8" × 7 3/4".

A cousin of the poet Ralph Waldo Emerson, the architect William
Ralph Emerson, originally from Illinois but based in Boston, was
John Calvin Steven's travel companion. This sketch highlights
the romantic and organic character of a European street. Many
of Emerson's works in the shingle style can be seen around Bar
Harbor in Maine. William Ralph Emerson (1833-1917), *Street Scene*.
Watercolor, 7 1/2″ x 13″.

Colter's buildings were instrumental in developing an architectural language that evoked the spirit of the American West. Mary Colter (1869-1958), *Drawing of Proposed Indian Garden Guesthouse*.

A white-clad Western lady, veiled against the sun, is the only human figure to be seen in this sloping street, lined with the geometrical, mud brick architecture of Morocco. Arnold William Brunner (1857-1925), *Tangiers*. Graphite, brush and watercolor on paper, 15 3/16" x 10 7/8".

A painting from Pries's travels. Pries was an influential teacher at
Washington University's School of Architecture and later became
director of the Art Institute of Seattle. Lionel H. Pries (1897-1968),
Corn in the River—Guanajuato, ca. 1946. Watercolor/tempera,
27″ x 38″.

Regional modernists such as Hartley were an important influence
on architects of the time. He was a specific influence on Pries.
Marsden Hartley (1877-1943), *New Mexico Recollection #12*, 1922-
1923. Oil on canvas. 30 ³/₁₆″ x 40 ¹/₁₆″.

The Architect Abroad

"When ideas are detached from the media used to transmit them, they are cut off from the historical forces that shape them."

E.L. Eisenstein, *Why Architects Draw*

A large part of the education of the architect has always been travel. Michaelangelo, Leonardo, Palladio expanded their universe as they traveled to Rome to study the architecture of what was then considered to be the height of Western civilization. As the cultural elites in Florence looked to the past for different precepts in art and architecture, they turned to the principles of Humanism, seeking a new understanding of the capacity of the human being for the creation of beauty—not God given, but through the spirit and hand of man. As witnessed in Rome, it was in our power as human beings to create beauty.

Throughout the following centuries, this quest for man's potential to create beauty became central not only to the development and formation of an architect, but to their transformation into professionals, believing that in order to be modern they must first understand the classical. England in the 18th century placed an important part of a proper education on the 'Grand Tour'. Architects, such as Inigo Jones, Robert Adam, and Sir John Soane, among others, sought to advance their architecture through this empirical understanding, visiting the monuments of the past in order to reinterpret for their own time—a right of passage required to be 'modern'. Eventually the English established several academies in Rome for the study of art and architecture.

These travels and studies were formalized as part of the education of the architect through the formation of the École des Beaux-Arts in Paris in 1648 (then known as the Académie des Beaux-Arts). Here, architects closely studied the classical ruins of Italy and in huge watercolor drawings, sometimes a dozen feet long, reproduced them in

Pries was deeply influenced by his experiences abroad. Here he captures the majesty of St. Peter's Basilica in Rome from an unexpected angle. Lionel H. Pries (1897-1968), *St. Peter's Basilica, Rome, Italy*, 1922. Watercolor, 15″ x 10″.

painstaking detail before they were allowed to conjecture their own detailed vision of how a structure may have been realized in its time. This combination of science, art and imagination became the instrument through which the architect would create modern works of their own for the next several generations.

The prestige of the École des Beaux-Arts attracted American students, beginning, in the 1840s, with the brothers Richard Morris Hunt and William Morris Hunt. Richard Morris Hunt returned to New York to become one of America's pre-eminent architects. William Morris Hunt's time in Paris was heavily influenced by the painters of the Barbizon School, forerunners of the Impressionists. Taken to America by Hunt, this movement inspired the dramatic landscape painting of the Hudson River School. Art historian Dorinda Evans writes that Hunt, along with James McNeill Whistler, believed that to paint something in its likeness was "the way to crush art and bring it down". In his 1885 lecture *Mr Whistler's "Ten O'Clock"* Whistler emphasized the importance of interpretation: "Nature contains the elements of color and form of all pictures—as the keyboard contains the notes of all music—but the artist is born to pick, and choose, and group with science, these elements, that the result may be beautiful." This sentiment made a profound impression on Winslow Homer.

The Cathedral
Over the Treetops
of the Plaza

Left: Goodhue left his Arts Club in Boston to travel and record the architecture and culture of Mexico. Bertram G. Goodhue (1869-1924), "The Cathedral over the Treetops of the Plaza" in *Mexican Memories: The Record of A Slight Sojourn Below the Yellow Rio Grande*.

Right: The patterns of Mackintosh's expressive work are reflective of his interpretations of his drawings of the coast of France. Charles Rennie Mackintosh (1868-1928), *Le Fort Mailly*, 1927. 14 ³/₈″ x 11 ¹/₈″.

After the Civil War, the success of the École des Beaux-Arts in Europe became the model for architectural education in the US, spawning ateliers that led to the foundation of America's first schools of architecture at MIT and the University of Columbia. In the manner of the Beaux-Arts, these schools gave science and the arts equal consideration.

While would-be architects now had more opportunity to study their chosen subject in the US, travel continued to remain highly important. This was even the case for architects of the Modern Movement who broke with the past to align their architecture with technology. Sketchbook and pencil were invariably part of their luggage, and the ability to learn about buildings through sketching and painting were critical to their formation as architects. If Walter Gropius had famously little aptitude for drawing, Le Corbusier, Louis Kahn and others considered avant garde in their work began by

drawing and studying abroad. Rome has shaped the contemporary architecture of Michael Graves, Robert Venturi, and even Peter Eisenman, among others.

Travel remains important to the education of most architects. Even the most technological and computer-forward architectural schools have programs abroad (most of them in Italy), and those that don't, seek to get their most exceptional students abroad somehow. Some programs allow for a few weeks in summer, while others, such as more classically based schools like Notre Dame, require their students to spend a year in Rome. Yet for many schools this practice became more one of tradition than of pedagogy, for once the students return to their studios the tools of sketching are often left in Rome with the ancients.

Then known as Charles Jeanneret, the artist studied and sketched historic buildings extensively before going on to become one of Europe's most influential modernists under the name of Le Corbusier.
Le Corbusier (1887-1965), *Tabernacle detail (design by Andrea Orcagna) at Orsanmichele, Florence*. Watercolor on paper, 5 11/16" x 4 3/4".

It is through travel that architects learn through seeing and understanding. As architects, we work within a continuum of architectural expression; some canonical and prescriptive, others quite incidental and inventive. Architecture has always been an expression of culture, time, and place. Through travel and experience we connect to architecture as a reaction to these important influences and continually apply those experiences towards ideas of our own. These empirical observations become the foundation of my response and expression as an architect.

As we draw from these lessons of the past, we put ourselves in the place of those who not only envisioned the buildings we see, but those who lived by crafting them. Ideas and physical manifestation are one. These buildings are also an expression of the ideals of a people, the values of a culture; how they see their environment, their political systems, their institutions, and their spirituality.

Drawing a building in person is different from seeing one through a photograph. It is a case of capture, versus response. In person, we can begin to observe a composition as a whole: the relationship of the elements of a structure. We can see the light striking the surface of a wall, the refraction of light in a shadow, the transformation of light as it passes through old glass, the texture of material. But it is even more than that. We also sense how a building belongs in its environment: its surroundings, the smell and dampness of the air, the sound of footsteps echoing through its chambers, the perceived warmth as you pass from a corridor into a courtyard: the expansion of space. You perceive how people react to the building. Do they scurry by without notice? Do they linger, do they sit in its shadow, do they run their fingers along its walls testing the textures left by those that chiseled its stone?

As I travel I seek to absorb these experiences, and like so many architects have done before me, I draw. Drawing is an instrument of memory. Drawing impresses upon my memory—my internal architectural library if you will—the details, the elements, and moments that a book or photograph could never capture. A photograph is a two-dimensional representation of a place which involves little active engagement on the part of the person taking it. As we draw we absorb so much more information. In the case of a building, we can begin to understand not only what the architect intended but also how the project looks in reality, and also how we would like it to be as a result of our experience of looking at it. We begin to see things that can't be seen. We feel. It is the experience of translation that engages all our senses, forming a memory. It is a cognitive interaction that registers and embeds itself within us and shapes our imagination; later this often reveals itself as an idea.

Left: Gilbert, another student at MIT's architectural school, joined McKim, Mead & White's office before establishing his own successful practice. Cass Gilbert (1859-1934), *Tower at Enkhuisen, Holland*, 1897. Watercolor and pencil on paper, 18 ³/₈″ x 12″.

Above: Mackintosh's work was intertwined with the allied arts. Here we see a painting from his travels along the French coast. Charles Rennie Mackintosh (1868-1928), *Little Bay, Port Vendres*. 15 ¹/₂″ x 15 ¹/₂″.

Gilbert's time studying drawing under MIT's Samuel Chamberlain no doubt influenced his sketchbook skills abroad. Travel sketchbooks were seminal to the American Renaissance and to an American architect's understanding of their place in that culture. Cass Gilbert (1859-1934), *Arch of Titus, Rome*, 1933. Watercolor and pencil on paper, 17 $^7/_8$" x 12".

02

The Stages
of Invention

Sense of Place

"One must get at the inside of the hill, the ledge, the tree, delve into its elemental nature."

Charles Herbert Woodbury, *Call of the Coast: Art Colonies of New England*

Architects have included the word *place*, or *genius loci*, in their lexicon for generations as the precept for buildings connecting with the location in which they are built. Yet this idea of place has become increasingly loosely regarded, as mass-produced materials are globally interchangeable and our buildings rarely respond to the cultural, material, or craft of a specific region. As architects seek to connect with the idea of 'local' we find there is much more to understanding a place than cartography.

A landscape is not just a location. It embraces all that a place is. It is the air, the water, the soil; it is the plants, trees, birds, animals, insects: all that surrounds it, and occupies it. It is the quality of light, the smell and sound. It is the people. It is both past and present—it is eternal. In its spirit it is an accounting of the history, the stories, the mythologies of a people and a place. A landscape isn't simply the appearance of a scene, but is connected to our histories, beliefs, struggles, and desires. Landscapes preside deep within us and bear meaning to who we believe we are as a people.

Edgar Payne reflects on the meaning that landscape has for the painter in *Composition of Outdoor Painting*: "Nature always challenges the capabilities of the imagination. Her variation in the line, form, color and ever-changing mood is infinitely beyond the variations resulting purely from invention or imagination."

As humans, we instinctively appreciate the 'scenographic', the way a beautiful landscape or part of a city is composed as though it were a picture in our mind. By painting nature we begin to understand the components of that picture: breadth, contrast, and focus. By studying that which we visually connect to through the observation of nature we may find a standard, or structure, or set of rules for understanding that appeal as we create

A watercolor of the stepwell of Jodhpur, a study capturing the drama of its scale and depth. It captures an architectural form unique to India, part of Michael's desire to faithfully record the spirit of a place. Michael G. Imber, *Steps of Jodhpur*.

as architects. By drawing the visual effects of nature we can begin to understand color, tone, shape, contour, structure, and focus. By drawing landscapes, we are recording our own visual experiences, seeking some essential truth in nature. Yet visual appearances are filtered through our own material perceptions founded in truth, yet realized through our imagination.

These observations are confirmed by the work of one of the greatest of Romantic painters, Eugene Delacroix. His phenomenal imagination drew inspiration from his travels. The starting point was his sketchbook. Here we see the germs of the ideas that became his masterpieces, in the form of studies. They show the places where his subjects lived; the landscapes that surrounded them; their culture, their customs, their dress, their mythology and symbolism. I have always enjoyed these sketchbooks far more than the large cinematic paintings that he produced from them. These sketchbooks were the research, the observation that eventually filled his paintings with authenticity. They explored the 'why' behind the paintings. It was by the intricate weaving of these observations into a rich and varied fabric that he was able to create the large, expressive canvases that captured the imaginations of his audiences.

It was noted that Monet would wear the sabots and native dress of Giverny in order to be *of* the place. As I sit to draw or paint a landscape *plein-air* there is an understanding that begins to form. I *feel* the place through all of my senses. I am present in that time and place. It is an empirical learning, an absorption through experience. All one's senses are engaged; sight, sound, touch, and smell. Maine artist Charles Woodbury would note, "one must paint in verbs, not nouns." in order to capture the true spirit of a place. It is this multi-sensory engagement that embeds into our minds a memory of a place. If we are fortunate enough to observe a place over time and season we may begin to understand through its transformations its interaction with time and eternity.

After World War II, American art shifted away from Emerson's bucolic view of the American future in our landscape. Industry became America's future.

Today the rugged coastline of Maine continues to attract artists to both its drama and the rich culture woven into its landscape. Contemporary Maine painters, like Bo Bartlett and Jamie (grandson of N.C. and son of Andrew) Wyeth's landscapes are full of metaphor and symbolism reflecting modern culture. Tom Curry paints a singular island outside his window. This island is painted in fog, in snow, in still light, and in wind and rain, in winter, in summer, in low tide and in high tide. There is a personality and spirit of place that begins to emerge—an understanding of an island that is intimate and deep, an understanding that is not a snapshot as we tend to see things but an eternal understanding.

Delacroix's paintings were informed by both his understanding of the culture and his own travel sketches. This composite page shows a landscape with a mosque in the background; various Arab figures; a sketch of a small mosque; and a Jewish man seated in shadow near a doorway. No part of the paper was wasted. Eugene Delacroix (1798-1863), "Landscape with mosque in the background and figures, sketch of a small mosque and Jewish man seated in shadow near a doorway" in *Album of North Africa and Spain*. Watercolor, pen and brown ink, 7 ³/₅" x 5".

Roman Bath, Potsdam

Above: Raindrops merging with paint. A thumbnail *esquisse* records the moment the heavens opened while Michael painted. Michael G. Imber, *Roman Bath, Potsdam*.

Right: This sketch attempts to capture the experience of being in Venice: architecture is important but so are the surrounding sounds and smells that make that place unique. The process of sketching fixes them in the memory. Michael G. Imber, *Venice, Italy*.

The chill in the air off the coast of Vancouver Island is given palpable form. Michael G. Imber, *Two trees, Vancouver*.

Clarence Town, Long Island '13

Above: A quick sketch of sculptural forms at St. Paul's Anglican Church showing the characteristic light stone against the brightness of the sky. Michael G. Imber, *Clarence Town. Long Island, Bahamas*.

Right: On a hot afternoon in France, the sun illuminates a winding, cobbled street. Michael G. Imber, *Street in La Coste Aix En Provence*.

A quick travel sketch done with two different mediums to achieve the desired effect. The sketch was first drawn in brown sepia pen then washed over with blue watercolor creating the warm and cool tones that compliment each other. Michael G. Imber, *Qutub Minar, Delhi*.

A drawing capturing the bright skies and sunbaked adobe of
Santa Fe. Michael G. Imber, *National Park Service, Santa Fe.*

Sitting with friends from the Whisky Watercolor Club, Michael had
to paint quickly as the incoming tide threatened to engulf them.
Michael G. Imber, *River Erne, Devon, England*.

Michael remembers "the heat on the back of my neck, the smell of
lavender from the adjacent field and the song of crickets sending
an electric current though the air." The sketch was made beneath
the intense summer sun of Southern France. Michael G. Imber,
Pont Julien.

Nobleman of the Phaleon Temple   2015
Aswan, Egypt

Michael paints people very rarely; only when they reflect something
of the character of the place and its architecture. Michael G. Imber,
Gentleman at Egyptian Temple.

A market scene in the village of Vandigar, Rajasthan, India.
Michael G. Imber, *Banara Market*.

Quick brush strokes in a sketchbook attempt to capture the energy of a village market in India. Michael G. Imber, *Banara Market*.

Palladio's Villa Capra, known as La Rotonda, is famous for having identical porticos on each of the four sides. Michael's study shows it in the landscape setting. Michael G. Imber, *Villa Capra*.

Above: A hut deep in the forest of the Adirondack Mountains.
Michael G. Imber, *Hagrid's Hut*.

Right: The shape of this dovecot was later used as an inspiration
for a library built in Texas. Michael uses every kind of sketchbook
and utensil and won't settle for just one format to express himself.
Neither of these depictions were painted on watercolor paper
hence the roughness of textures. Michael G. Imber, *Le Pigeonner*.

Le Pigeonnier
du Château Bagnols

A quick impression of Soho Square. What appears to be a gardener's hut in the 'Tudorbethan' style is the entrance to an underground substation built by the Charing Cross Electricity Company in the 1920s. Michael G. Imber, *Soho Square, London*. 5 ½" x 6 ¼".

Park Monceau, Paris

Park Monsieur in a snowstorm. The rotunda of 1787 is one of the
barrières designed by Claude-Nicolas Ledoux for the collection of
taxes by the *fermiers généraux* (tax farmers); they were part of a wall
commissioned by the chemist Antoine Lavoisier, who was himself
a *fermier général* and guillotined during the French Revolution.
Michael G. Imber, *Park Monsieur, France*.

ISI BEAN CENTER   MGI '12

The Cart of Fate

"The architect engaged his audience and brought them,
honestly and without coercion, to want what he wanted."

William Hubbard, *Complicity and Conviction: Steps toward an Architecture of Convention*

Architecture is a long process: a series of continual negotiations from conception to completion of construction. An idea forms and, as the architect Allan Greenberg believes, immediate diplomacy begins. The *charrette* allows an architect to communicate ideas quickly and to build a consensus that is lasting for the duration of the project.

Charrette is a French term for the cart used to collect the final drawings of the students of the École des Beaux-Arts. Lore has it, the students would be so furiously working on the completion of their drawings that they would fling themselves onto the cart and draw as it rambled down the cobbled street to judgment. The anecdote rings true for the fast pace of an architectural *charrette* today. As architects we use what we call the *charrette* process to arrive at a solution (and judgment of that solution) as quickly as possible, while the client is flung into our cart with us.

Architecture is unique among the arts: in only the rarest of occasions can it be realized by a single person. In the Middle Ages buildings rose slowly from the ground as a collaboration between master masons, master carpenters, and other trades. At the dawn of the Renaissance, drawing revolutionized architecture. It allowed architects to work out their ideas in advance of construction; they could carry them around with them and show them to clients. Architecture became more intellectual, less of a craft. The old trial-and-error approach was replaced by more scientific methods. Even so, the best architects of the Renaissance and later centuries did not ignore the masons, carpenters, bricklayers, glaziers, smiths, and other practical people with whom they worked. In some cases they took their advice.

A quick *esquisse* drawing during a *charrette* to illustrate the vision of a client. Michael G. Imber, *ISI Bean Center*.

Today, a large number of people with different skills are involved in the construction of major buildings. The *charrette* is a means of engaging all these many players at once. It often involves not only the architect and their consultants, but also the client, the client's representatives, and interested parties often including the community itself. These are intensive exercises, often lasting only a few days, with the architects working long hours to understand, rationalize, deduce, and produce solutions as quickly as possible. After the research required to understand the cultural and physical landscape in which we are to build, ideas flow through reams of paper, stopping at intervals for testing and client feedback, towards a solution in which everyone concurs. For architects, sketches allow for possibilities. Initial rough sketches are left open-ended and therefore have more possible outcomes. As a sketch develops, those outcomes become more defined. A sketch allows an architect to stand in judgment of the possibilities and allows him to discern, determine, and guide the final results.

I have traveled to many places throughout the United States and the world to *charrette* with other talented architects, planners, and clients. They have each been an intensive process of learning and adaptation before the eventual arrival at conclusions and consensus. The result has been some beautiful and long-lasting built environments. Our role is always primarily that of the architectural 'hit team', dropping in to understand and coalesce the essence of a landscape and culture into an architectural expression true to the spirit of the place. We are often thrown into the 'cart', drawing furiously for many hours on end. Fascinatingly, the sketches that are conceptualized often become the very seed of authenticity to be built into a lasting community.

Left: As is so often the case, on a trip to help design a new Spanish town, Michael found himself to be in a very different time zone, so he spent the early hours of the morning sketching the hilltop village you can see in the distance. Michael G. Imber, *Arcos de la Frontera*.

Above: After exploring and adjusting to the building traditions of Spanish villages of the Pueblo Blancos region of Spain, a new town street was designed with a variety of housing types. Michael G. Imber, *Arcos Streetscape, Spain*.

A study aiming to develop an architectural
language for a new town in the Bahamas.
Michael G. Imber, *The Island House,
Harbor Hotel*.

E ISLAND HOUSE

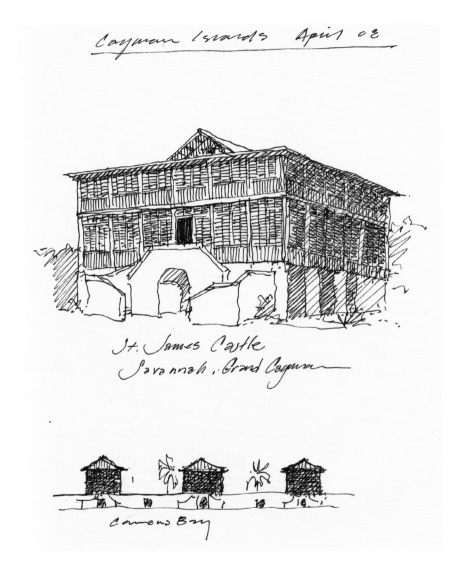

Cayman Islands   April 02

St. James Castle
Savannah, Grand Cayman

Cayman Bay

A concept for housing in the Cayman Islands. Michael G. Imber,
Caymen Islands.

A rough conceptualisation in pen of courtyard housing. Michael G.
Imber, *Caymen Islands*.

A vision for the future of Biloxi, Mississippi after Hurricane Katrina.
Michael G. Imber, *Biloxi, Mississippi*.

Re-envisioning the Gold Coast of Mississippi after Hurricane Katrina.
Michael G. Imber, *Bon Secour, Mississippi*.

A housing project for Inverness, Scotland.
Like the studies on previous pages,
this drawing was conceived from the
cultural DNA of its region, to develop an
architectural code for the building of new
towns. Michael G. Imber, *Castlestuart Park*.

One of a series of studies of the different forms a new restaurant
might take in the Bahamas. Michael G. Imber, *Restaurant, Lyford
Cay Bahamas*.

A study of a small hotel on Abaco Island. Michael G. Imber,
Schooner Bay Yacht Club.

A very quick concept for a sorority house at the University of Arkansas. Michael G. Imber, *Delta Gamma Sorority, University of Arkansas*.

A sorority headquarters in Ohio. Michael G. Imber, *Delta Gamma HQ, Ohio*.

Ideals on Paper

"One of the joys of being an architect is the exhilaration that comes from drawing—your hand and the pencil it holds are an extension of your creative thought process"

Deborah Berke, Dean of Yale School of Architecture

We learn the language of drawing in childhood. We can hold a crayon and apply it to paper even before we can speak. At an early age this visual language develops alongside our verbal expression. As soon as a child can take an instrument and make a mark, they enthusiastically embrace the ability to express themselves. Color often explodes on paper as expressions of ideas, a synthesis of their experiences, and of their imagination. In those who eventually become architects, that ability to materialize ideas on paper has been central to professional discourse and in the practice of architecture.

The most evolved form of drawing for the architect is the presentation drawing. This is a highly finished work that enables the client and anyone else interested in a building project to visualize what it will look like when completed. It errs towards idealization in some cases, but that only underlines the fundamentally romantic nature of architecture. It is the vision in all of its potential. The presentation drawing shows what is possible before the architect's vision has been compromised by the harsh realities of budget and other forces. In this way it is more than the name implies. It is a way to connect us to the past, to the landscape, and to the materiality of craft. Most importantly, it connects us to the continuum of the practice of architecture. Architecture exists in two worlds: the built and the imagined. Presentation drawings, by suggesting possibilities rather than defining them with technological precision, allow the client to enter the exciting realm that lies between the idea and the finished project. Their imagination can come into play alongside that of the architect.

A watercolor presentation for a project in Montecito, California. Michael G. Imber, *Montecito, California*.

This illustrates the distinction between art and illustration. Many architects illustrate their projects through rendering. This is a particularly common practice today given the use of computer rendering and modeling programs that simulate detailed materials in realistic light and shadow. While these drawings wish to convey information of a space or of a form, they may also extend to the simulation of reality; a built reality where drawings leave no room for the imagination, no room for the viewer to insert themselves into the moment. Art on the other hand is much like poetry. It allows room for the mind to wander between the lines, to create its own journey and even conclusions within the picture. It allows the viewer to project their own desires, to live in it as they imagine themselves living. It not only creates a picture of a thing, it transports us to experience emotively. In fact, during the Renaissance there remained a debate on whether art or poetry was the best connection of man to nature.

Much more has been conceptualized by architects than ever built. For centuries they have expressed ideas through drawing. Art connects us to our humanity. Leonardo da Vinci would try to capture not merely just a form in a gesture, but seek to convey the emotional intent behind the gesture. Computer presentation renderings may be technically perfect, or highly realistic, but they lack the human dimension.

The beginning of architectural drawing in practice dates from the 15th century. During the Renaissance, from Alberti and Leonardo da Vinci to Vasari, architecture occupied a place between craft and art. For the first time the "why" beyond the "how" in building

This pencil drawing depicts the texture of the stone ranch house, an effect which could not be achieved in watercolor. Michael G. Imber, *Texas Ranch House*.

was being defined. Before he was an artist, and before he was an architect, Leonardo was first an observer of the world, spending hours observing eddies in a stream, a feather in the wind, or the refraction of light. This ability to observe and to express in drawing gave rise to a new breed of architect and a much greater variety of ideas to be employed by builders. It was a cornerstone for a renaissance in thinking. Since that time, drawing has always been the foundation of what it means to be an architect.

It was the ability to draw that elevated architects above master masons and master carpenters, however skilled they might be. Drawing was the means by which they could visualize an unbuilt project, then communicate their idea to both clients and builders. The better their mastery of this art, the more accurately they could relay what they had in their mind. In this, architects were similar to artists, although their sphere of operation was different. The fruit of their imaginations would, they hoped, eventually be constructed to create forms and spaces that might shape an environment or culture for generations. Ideas that began as fleeting impressions on the mind were captured through drawing and given solidity and permanence.

Previous spread: Watercolor is the best way to express this white plaster building, whose walls contrast strongly with the pantile roof. Michael G. Imber, *Dos Rios Lake Elevation*.

Above: A quick pencil sketch painted with watercolor. Michael G. Imber, *Dos Rios Guest House*.

A sketchbook concept of a studio in the woods of Maine.
Michael G. Imber, *Maine Tower*.

Schematic design drawings of a house on the Sea of Cortez.
The colored paper allowed for the expression of the building's
white plaster in gouache. Michael G. Imber, *Casa Dauphine,
Sea of Cortez, Baja, Mexico*.

After a 1940s ranch compound burned down, the new ranch house
which replaced it was meant to evoke a similar era to the original.
This is expressed in the technique chosen for this watercolor.
Michael G. Imber, *Rancho Del Cielo, West Texas*.

Attempting to replicate Bertram Goodhue's pen and ink technique
was also a study in how to direct the eye through the composition of
the drawing as well as leading the eye purposely to different elements
of the architecture. Michael G. Imber, *Ranch House in Texas*.

The watercolor study of this artist studio in Texas was meant to have
a more artistic expression reflective of the client. Michael G. Imber,
Classical Artist Studio, Austin, Texas.

The dark sky of an approaching rainstorm expresses the vast open space surrounding a ranch in South Texas. Michael G. Imber, *Hacienda Tortuga*.

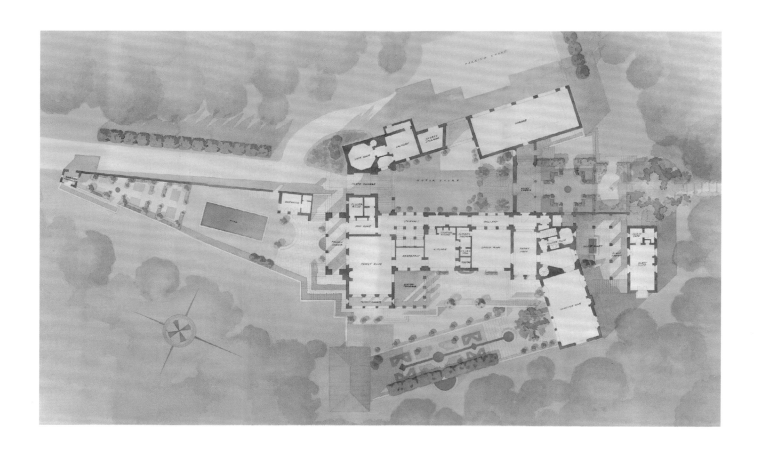

Previous spread: Form and landscape are unified within a single palette using a technique inspired by the Italian garden studies of Shepherd and Jellicoe. Michael G. Imber, *Mount Larson, East Elevation*.

Above: Floor plan of the building on Mount Larson (previous spread) showing each part of the property and its outbuildings. Michael G. Imber, *Mount Larson, Floor Plan*.

Right: A rendering of a timber frame library inspired by a French dovecote. Mac White, *Timber Frame Library*.

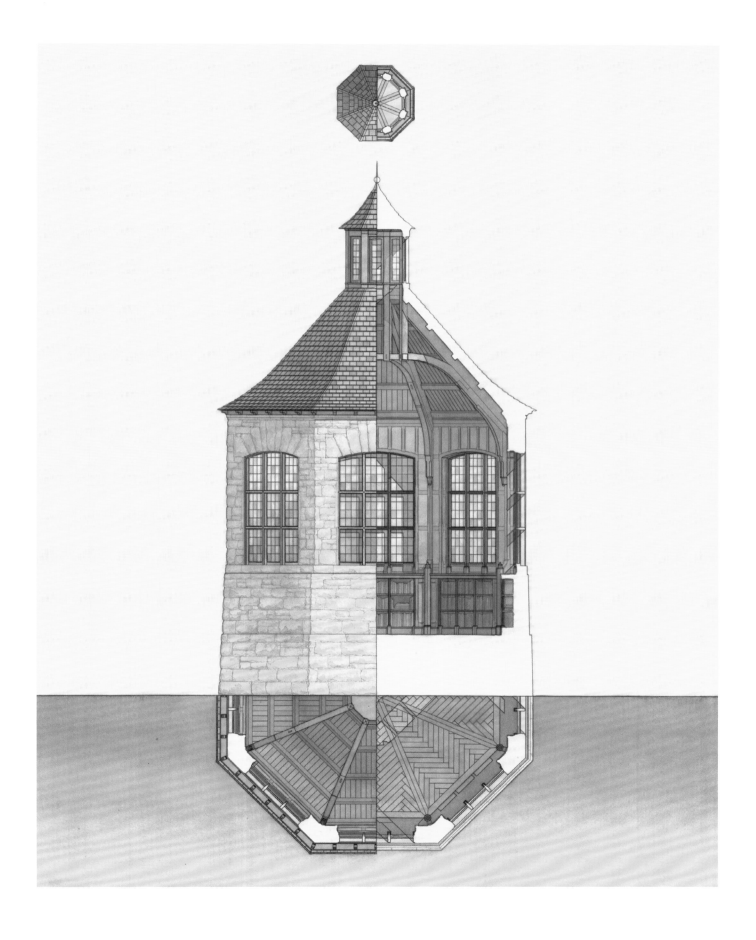

A Texas ranch house sits on a cliff in a dramatic landscape.
Michael G. Imber, *Texas Ranch Home Set on a Cliff*.

A schematic rendering of a stable set in an almost dreamlike forest.
Anton Glikin, *Stable, Montana*.

A watercolor rendering of a chapel for a college campus in Ojai,
California. Michael G. Imber, *Thomas Aquinas*.

An interior perspective drawing for a seminary chapel in North
Carolina showing high vaulted ceilings and ornate woodcarving.
Mac White, *Seminary Chapel Interior, North Carolina*.

Drawing in Practice

"The craft of drawing has traditionally been the hallmark of the architect. Involving as it does the mind, the eye and the hand, it builds understanding of its object on several levels. An idea that originates in the mind is expressed by the hand in such a way that the visible result is the product of both thought and action."

David Ross Scheer, *The Death of Drawing: Architecture in an Age of Simulation*

Working drawings have always been seen as the technical side of practice—the nuts and bolts of architecture—and little to do with art. Yet working drawings begin at conceptualization and can never be disassociated from the revelation of that idea. Form and space begin to take shape early and, as drawings progress, the character and personality begin to take shape, giving a greater grain of information as they develop. The integrity of the string of connected decisions that creates a building starts with the first conceptual sketch.

Each consecutive sketch, drawing, and decision in the process goes back to reinforcing that initial expression of the idea. Often, initial ideas present themselves as gestures. Gestures may be left open-ended, or a line, or scribble left for resolution later. This allows the free flow of thought to continue uninterrupted. Gestures may be bold or fine depending on the instrument. Large bold pencils or markers lend themselves to quick, broad gestures; while finer pens slow the thought process down and require greater intent. Even the texture of the paper can help guide the formation of an idea. Marks may be made without any intent at all, but merely to push the mind forward seeking patterns or resolutions. Layers can be built upon, each subsequently bringing the idea into focus. Early in the process we begin to explore relationships to the landscape and to the local culture, the expression of form the building will take, its materiality, and most

Sepia pen and watercolor sketch for a ranch addition in Texas. The watercolor wash over the ink allows it to bleed, illuminating details of the house and landscape. Michael G. Imber, *T-Anchor Ranch*.

importantly, the experiences it will shape. Details of elements follow as a derivative of the base understanding that formed the idea and solution: a porch creating a foil to a mass, or a buttress connecting to the earth, or a chimney placed to sweep the eye in a particular direction. Even the description of the size, form, and pattern of stone falls within this process of decision making.

Often, different tools are combined. Traditionally it would be drawing and physical models of clay, wood, or plaster. Computers weren't the first mechanical tools architects used for drawing. There have been clever new devices to assist the architect graphically since the ancient Greeks. Today, the computer has expanded those tools to AutoCad, 3D computer models, 3D prints, and, of course, computer simulation. These are often used in tandem to test ideas, set up given frameworks, or resolve complex modeling. Using these tools without sketching or drawing often forces the designer into a linear process rather than an iterative process that spirals into a solution, or multiple solutions. Often, computers are used in tandem with hand drawing, and even some drawings use a combination of hand and machine as the final expression.

Decisions and artistic adjustments do not end with design. Working drawings, or construction documents, continue the creative process. Collaboration of the vision becomes increasingly important as the team begins the process of laying down within drawing the necessary information for construction. As David Ross Scheer suggests, there is a profound relationship between the vision of the artist and the vision of the builder: "In a well-made set of working drawings, builders can see the work of a master craftsman, analogous to the mastery they have achieved in their own crafts." A team of architects and draftsmen come together to begin to arrange the components of a building into a whole. This process of envisioning how each element relates to and reinforces the next, builds, piece by piece, the two-dimensional drawings.

These drawings start with manipulating a concept or scheme into realistic buildable elements. Through a process of design development, the relationships and tectonics of each component must be tested, adjusted, and refined to reinforce the whole. Each

Left: A quick thumbnail *esquisse* of a ranch in Texas. Michael G. Imber, *Independence Horse Farm Ranch*.

Right: This perspective was partly generated on computer but informed by Lenahan's understanding of hand-rendering techniques. Jim Lenahan, *Pedernales Interior*.

line ensures a greater integrity of the idea towards the realization. A small community of engineers and consultants come into play, and ideas and concepts are further tested, challenged, integrated, and reinforced.

Although highly technical at this stage, the art of drawing does not stop here. The understanding of form and composition, scale and detail must be transferred from both the knowledge and imagination of the draftsman into documents that are precise and buildable. Elements that must be manufactured (or those that will be hand-crafted) must be described to a degree that another may understand the material's shape and substance in order to be produced in line with the architectural vision as a whole. Purpose and intent are conveyed to the craftsman and the maker. The architect must understand how the disparate parts—often made great distances apart—will come together with harmony and integrity.

These drawings are not merely technical but may be artistic in their own right, even when produced on computers. Line weights, composition, and the clarity of instruction are all part of the architect's artistic skill. As in writing or poetry, conveying a complex set of information in the simplest and most elegant way is the highest form of the art. Whether on paper or on a computer screen, the architect weaves his magic, translating the images in his mind into a form that others can see, study, and enjoy. Architectural drawings can be beautiful, even expressive. Yet ultimately they are the means to a single end: to translate an idea from mind into matter.

Michael uses conceptual drawings to work out the structure
of a building, rather like thinking on paper. Michael G. Imber,
Conceptual Drawing.

Concept sketch for a golf clubhouse in the Texas Hill Country,
experimenting with pen hatching and watercolor. Impressions taken
briefly in the field later come together in more considered drawings.
Michael G. Imber, *Conceptual Drawing*.

Renderings are meant to evoke the landscapes in which we build. This ranch house sits atop a rugged limestone bluff overlooking a state park in Texas. The painting is informed by a real-life understanding of how light and shadow work in nature. Sam Usle, *Pedernales Ranch Sitting on a Bluff*.

A quick conceptual sketch for a house on Long Island, Bahamas.
Michael G. Imber, *Home in the Bahamas*.

Michael's first visit to a site in Telluride, Colorado, was after a significant snowstorm. The *esquisse* for the project reflected that experience. Michael G. Imber, *Telluride, Colorado*.

One of a series of quick pencil sketches illustrating the sequence
of scenes encountered in a new country estate. Andrew Gander,
Austin Equestrian Estate Stable.

A sketch done as a series of sequencing moments moving through the grounds of an estate. Andrew Gander, *Austin Equestrian Estate Guest House*.

Above: Concept sketch for a library scheme in Texas showing the fireplace front-on. The spiral staircase allows access to a balcony, creating a second level within the room, while maintaining the high ceiling. Andrew Gander, *Austin Equestrian Estate Library*.

Right: The library from another angle. A more detailed painting reveals special features in the room: the painted figures on the ceiling, the dramatic light fixture, and generous windows. Sam Usle, *Austin Equestrian Estate Library*.

A pen and ink concept for a proposed pumphouse, produced
quickly in the field. Michael G. Imber, *Pump House*.

A sketch illustrating an entry sequence to a proposed lodge in
Montana. The tall pines lining the driveway provide a scenic route
to the house. Michael G. Imber, *Montana Main House Approach*.

A thumbnail conceptual study sketch for a South Texas ranch.
Michael G. Imber, *Two Rivers Ranch*.

A small watercolor sketch for a ranch chapel in Texas.
Michael G. Imber, *Chapel on Hill*.

Watercolors of conceptualized buildings often reflect the
landscapes in which they are to be built. Michael G. Imber,
Rock House.

A conceptual sketch for a solitary tower for the South Padre
National Seashore in Texas. The land and sky reflect a range of
different color tones. Michael G. Imber, *Corpus Christi Tower,
Padre Island National Seashore*.

03

In the Studio

A Culture at Work

"Don't talk about it, draw it."

Edwin Lutyens

My first real renderings were produced while in the office of Allan Greenberg. It was the first time I had colleagues referencing Beaux-Arts renderings and the drawings of 19th-century architects. In school we referenced the work of contemporaries, but here we were looking at the best architectural renderings ever produced by the masters of the 18th and 19th centuries. This not only opened our eyes to the possibilities of expression, but also connected us to the minds and hands of those architects of the past.

However, this lineage had been broken. We now had to teach ourselves, practicing watercolor and pen and ink at home until we were willing to render an important project in the office. These early efforts in the 1980s, with colleagues like Michael Lykoudis, Duncan Stroik, and Michael Mesko, ended up as an important part of the pedagogy of The University of Notre Dame's Architectural program and the Institute of Classical Architecture's Grand Academy. My studio mates moved on to their careers in education: Michael Mesko instrumental in the Institute's Grand Academy, and Duncan Stroik as a professor at Notre Dame under Michael Lykoudis as dean of the College of Architecture, following the path set forth for the school by the former dean, Thomas Gordon Smith, teaching the principles of classical architecture and its tools of practice.

As a studio today, we continue to value these principles as well as valuing the importance of hand-drawing. As the practice proved formative in my growth as an architect, I wished to create a studio built on the foundation of the craft of drawing—not just rendering—as an art in, and of, itself towards a means of expression, emotion, and the spirit of an idea; a place in which culture, history, and the craft of the architect lived within our drawings. Many in our studio have a background in drawing, either having loved it for a long time, or having come from an architectural program such as Notre Dame where drawing is seen as an important part of the architectural process.

Plein-air watercolor with Texas ICAA led by Stephen Harby at Mission San Jose. Mac White, *Mission San Jose*.

We encourage drawing in both the process as well as practice. Loose sketches and drawings leave more to the imagination than a computer rendering. Drawing allows the viewer more ownership of what is being perceived, both in its possibilities, and as a perceived reality. Many architects both manage and build the projects that they have personally done renderings or hand-drawings of. This lends a certain integrity to a project: a line, if you will, from the idea to the realization. I believe this is the basis for integrity, helping to generate a certain human spirit in a building. It is what connects what is within us to what we create. These architects are also able to convey their ideas or concepts directly to a builder or a client, either with some quick lines in a sketchbook, or an elaborate sketch on a 2 x 4 scrap from the jobsite. It is an instant conveyance of the idea, intent, or solution.

This drawing culture persists in what is known as the MGIA Sketch Club. Every Friday, over breakfast tacos (a San Antonio tradition), a group gathers in the back room of the office. Having chosen a subject, such as a tree, a landmark building, or an object they will set a timer for either ten, fifteen, or twenty minutes. Often they look at the handwork of well-known artists and architects, such as Arthur Guptill and John Ruskin. As they study they discover the way they moved their pencil, pen, or brush, how they conveyed the material qualities of light shimmering through a shadow. Some of the resulting sketches are brilliant, some less so. But the point is not to create masterpieces. Genius is not the goal. The point of the exercise is to develop technique for expression, to continue to form better hand-eye coordination, to develop control, precision, and establish purpose of line. In essence, to develop their graphic language skills to the point that their thoughts are fluent through the instrument of a pen, pencil, or brush.

Left: While under the auspices of Alan Greenberg, Michael not only learned about the continuum of architectural language, but about how it could be expressed. This drawing was inspired by Bertram G. Goodhue. Michael G. Imber, *Connecticut Manor*.

Right: Sketches like this help inform techniques within the office. The Sketch Club meets every week to practice their skills using illustrations of traditional artists to inspire them. Arthur L. Guptill (1891-1956), "Illustration" from *Renderings in Pen and Ink*.

These exercises not only tap into the mind of the architect, coordinating their thoughts and ideas, but inform the architect's decision-making process through the development of drawings, and through construction. Attention to detail becomes acute, and the eye more aware of the nature of things.

It is important for architects to sketch impressions of buildings but also the landscapes in which these buildings are built, referred to by John Calvin Stevens as "seeing the site." Alice Arnn, *West Texas from the Bus*.

Above: During the morning exercises of the Sketch Club, a timer would be set for 15 minutes, and students would be given a subject to do a quick sketch of. Mind-hand coordination, relating visual information through physical motion, becomes an instant reflex. Sketch Club. Andrew Gander.

Right: A compositional vignette study done with pen and ink on toned paper. Andrew Gander, *San Antonio Medical Arts Building*.

A 15-minute study of the Tower Life Building as seen from the San Antonio Riverwalk. The pencil hatching captures the light reflecting off the surface of the water. Andrew Gander. Sketch Club. Graphite on paper.

Sketch Club students would try out their techniques on small 4″ x 5″
notecards until it became an everyday language. In this sketch the
Austin Tower is theatrically defined by the negative shading around
it. Andrew Gander, *University of Texas at Austin Tower*.

A formal watercolor drawing. Andrew Gander, *Gibbs Building*.

Above: A watercolor sketch of a Russian pavilion in winter, for the 2004 Michael G. Imber, Architects Christmas card. Mac White, *Winter in Pavlovsk*.

Right: A watercolor of the Lyceum Theater in New York City done as a series of paintings on New York. Mac White, *Lyceum*.

This view of St. Philip's Church was completed after an MGIA office retreat and highlights the building's prominent spire seen from Church Street. Jim Lenahan, *Charleston*. Mixed media.

The McNay Art Museum in San Antonio expressed with a limited
color palette to showcase the Spanish revival details and evoke the
1920s design. Jim Lenahan, *McNay*. Mixed media.

A pen and ink wash study of her favorite church in Rome.
Maureen Clarke, *Santa Maria Della Pace*.

Watercolor of Columbia Circle in New York City, done as a series of
paintings in the city. Mac White, *Columbus Circle*.

Griffith Observatory sketch done as part of the Southern California
ICAA "Sketch at Home Together" during Covid lockdown. Mac
White, *Griffith Observatory*.

This view of Pasadena City Hall was sketched after a site visit working on a nearby residence. Most of the linework was completed on the plane trip from photo reference. Jim Lenahan, *Pasadena Town Hall*. Mixed media.

Mission San Jose in San Antonio. A Spanish frontier mission, founded
in 1720. Luis Quiñonez, *Mission San Jose*.

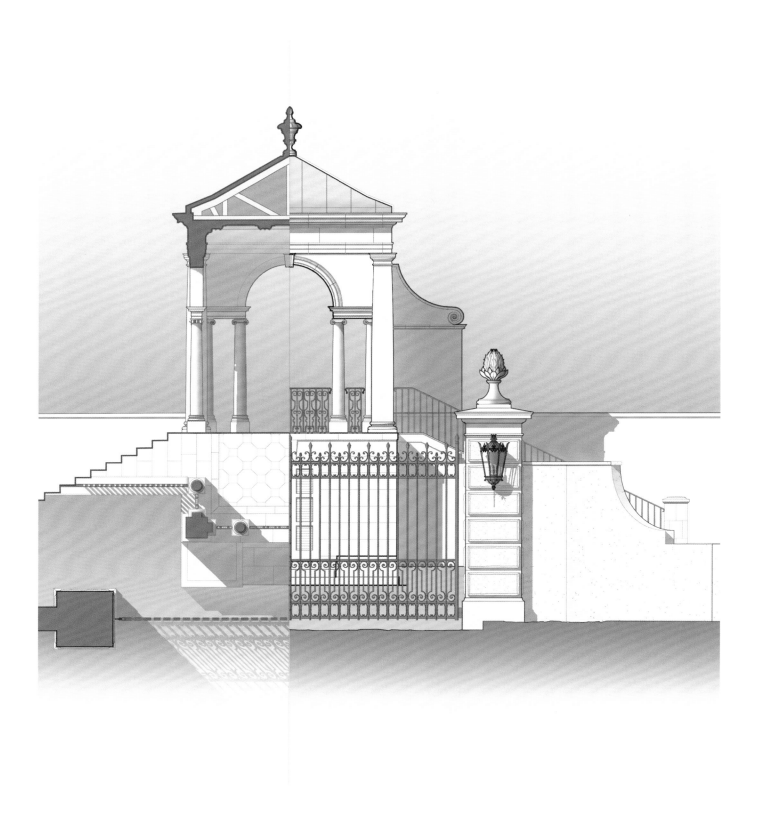

Lessons from the Drawing Board

"Pencil notes or sketches are experiments in solving problems, exercising the mental faculties and developing facility with the hand. Mental ideas are brought to visuality and crystalized and, at the same time, the hand is trained to work in unison with the brain."

Edgar Payne, *Composition of Outdoor Painting*

It has always been rare for the principal of a large architectural office to do renderings himself, and this is particularly true today. However there is a reason why I still do renderings. They are not merely for illustrating a project to a client, they are an integral part of the design process. As discussed, the material realization of an idea begins with a concept drawing. The concept gets refined through an iterative process over trace; the idea congealing, shifting, refining, resolving until there is form, space, material, and shaped experiences that are indicative of the project brief. These conceptual drawings then typically go to a team member who draws it in AutoCad, so that it can be "drafted" on the computer. Although this is a computer process, this is not simulation; we still consider this representational drawing, but merely with a different tool. Other programs are sometimes used to create 3D drawings to resolve and further study certain conditions; they can be extraordinarily useful. But we are still drawing, and the result often creates the base drawings for renderings, renderings being drawings of higher complexity—created with greater precision—than hand sketches.

An analytique of a gatehouse for an estate in San Antonio expressed in one architectural drawing: elevation, section and floorplan. Michael Chang, *Magnolia Hill Folly*.

Once the rough concept has been laid out in a drawing with measurement and precision, I often re-enter the process of the presentation of the drawings. It is here that, as an architect, I am able to manipulate the design into a drawing form that a builder can measure and use. I can begin to better understand and nuance the design through a process of discovery. As in understanding the natural world, I begin to comprehend light and shadow, reflection and refraction of light, form, scale, composition, and focus. I can begin to manipulate small but important aspects of the design: a gentle sweep of a roof tile; the breadth and weight of a chimney; the way a buttress connects a form to the landscape. Even more so, I can begin to study material. It is here that I select the stone, understand the mix of its coloration, its size, its pattern, its modulation and weight. Does it change scale? Does it become more refined or more rugged in its character? This is not just a drawing, it is the point at which I can enter the mind of the mason; understand his hand and how each stone will lay upon the next; the combination of shapes, the coloration, and pattern. It becomes the road map that will inform the mason's sample, then mock-up, and eventually the final wall. It is an understanding of making that I will arrive at while in the process of drawing. It is the idea realized on paper. We often return to this original drawing to ensure the process of creation is in keeping with the vision.

These drawings are an important part of the design process, not merely drawings to convey to a client how their building may appear, but as a continued process of discovery and revelation of the potential of the material, and form of the building. Relationships begin here that will inform the development of the construction documents, material specification, and eventually material mockups in the field to approximate the nuance the drawing sought to achieve.

I specifically draw conceptual floor plans first by hand. As I draw the thickness of the walls, the adjacencies, and modulation of form and space, they are not just two-dimensional lines on paper. I am feeling. I am seeing space and understanding the experience as I wander the halls of the drawing. I am invested with every line as it begins to build into a sequence of rooms with import of emotion and materiality. As with painting, nearly *all* my senses are involved with this process. I am seeing the reflection of light, feeling the texture of the walls and floor, hearing the echo between spaces, and smelling the warm tones of the wax—carrying attention to a small purposeful detail or moment. I am living in the drawing and I am building in my mind.

These rooms are at once interlocked with the vision of the mass and forms of the architecture. The width of a room shapes the height and pitch of the roof. A nook may form a hinge as a wall swings to embrace a view, or shape an outdoor room to capture the summer breeze. Fenestration creates scale and illumination of space in the interior, while framing a view to a particular point in the landscape. A corner sharpens to anchor a wall to a hillside. All of this together is formed while the pencil travels over the paper. The mind wanders the rooms, flying overhead above the forms of the roof, sequencing an arrival point by point to a purposeful experience.

For Michael, teasing the idea from the mind onto paper starts with thumbnail sketches like these, before becoming a more sophisticated image. Michael G. Imber, *Last Dollar Ranch*.

An aerial perspective of the architecture and its relationship to
shapes within the landscape, and a study of the form and elevation
to scale. Michael G. Imber, *Last Dollar Ranch*.

A pencil study of the main mass of the lodge bringing the concept
into appropriate scale. Michael G. Imber, *Last Dollar Ranch*.

A pencil rendering of the final design for a ranch on a mountain in
Telluride. The ranch was built from local stone mined from the site
itself. Michael G. Imber, *Last Dollar Ranch*.

Left: A test watercolor working out the palette prior to executing the formal rendering. Michael G. Imber, *Mount Larson*.

Above: An early *esquisse* of the guesthouse and garage was done to work out the architectural language before moving on to the main house. Michael G. Imber, *Mount Larson*.

ELEVATION STUDY
MANLY RESIDENCE AT GRIFFER

Final watercolor presentation of the main building set amongst
tall pines. Mac White, *Mount Larson*.

The initial study of a landscape. The watercolors conjure the
shimmering heat of the desert. Michael G. Imber, *King Hart
Ranch Barn*.

Tower Study   King Hart Ranch

An image of a tower built to watch storms, known as "Blue Northers", as they roll across the plain. Even the most severe storms could be watched safely from the vantage of the tower. Michael G. Imber, *King Hart Ranch Tower*.

A conceptual watercolor of the courtyard below the tower.
Michael G. Imber, *King Hart Ranch Court Yard*.

A rendering of the storm tower showing the
wine cellar built beneath, doubling up as a storm
shelter. The cellar is accessible from the tower so
that during storms it can be reached without the
need to venture outside. Michael G. Imber, *King
Hart Ranch Section*.

A conceptual sketch of a small cottage in the San Francisco Bay area.
Michael G. Imber, *Burlingame*.

Michael's initial conceptual *esquisse* (left) was designed to be
built using shingle, based on the architectural traditions of the San
Francisco Bay area. The client decided to go with a different material
in the final construction, but the formal elements remained the same.
Jim Lenahan, *Burlingame*.

A study of early Texas architecture to help inform the language before they begin designing. Michael G. Imber, *Rancho Sabino Grande Precedent Study*.

A pencil and watercolor study of a small, traditional South Texas
ranch house, as a precedent for a modern ranch house. Michael G.
Imber, *Rancho Sabino Grande Precedent Study*.

Above: The original *charrette* concept drawn during meetings with
the client. Michael G. Imber, *St. Joseph Seminary*.

Right: White's rendering of the tower for the seminary, showing its
elegant arched tympanum. Mac White, *St. Joseph Seminary*.

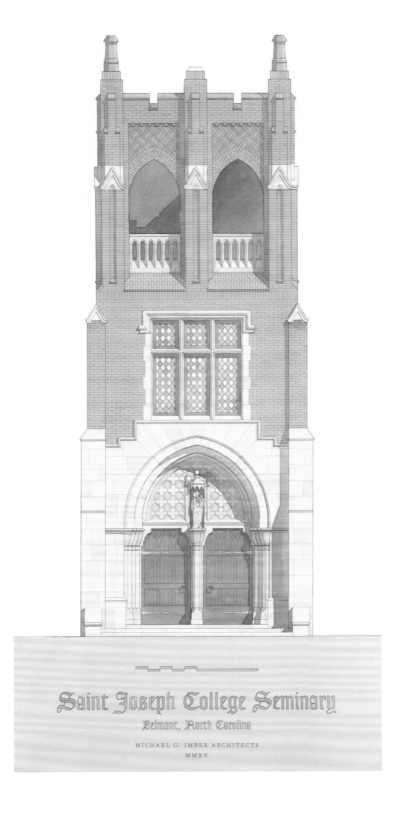

Saint Joseph College Seminary

Belmont, North Carolina

MICHAEL G. IMBER ARCHITECTS

MMXV

An aerial watercolor of the seminary in North Carolina.
Elizabeth LaDuke, *St. Joseph Seminary Aerial*.

The final presentation of the concept before it was built: a linear
process from initial *esquisse*, to conceptual renderings and
watercolors, to the final artwork. Andre Junget, *St. Joseph Seminary*.

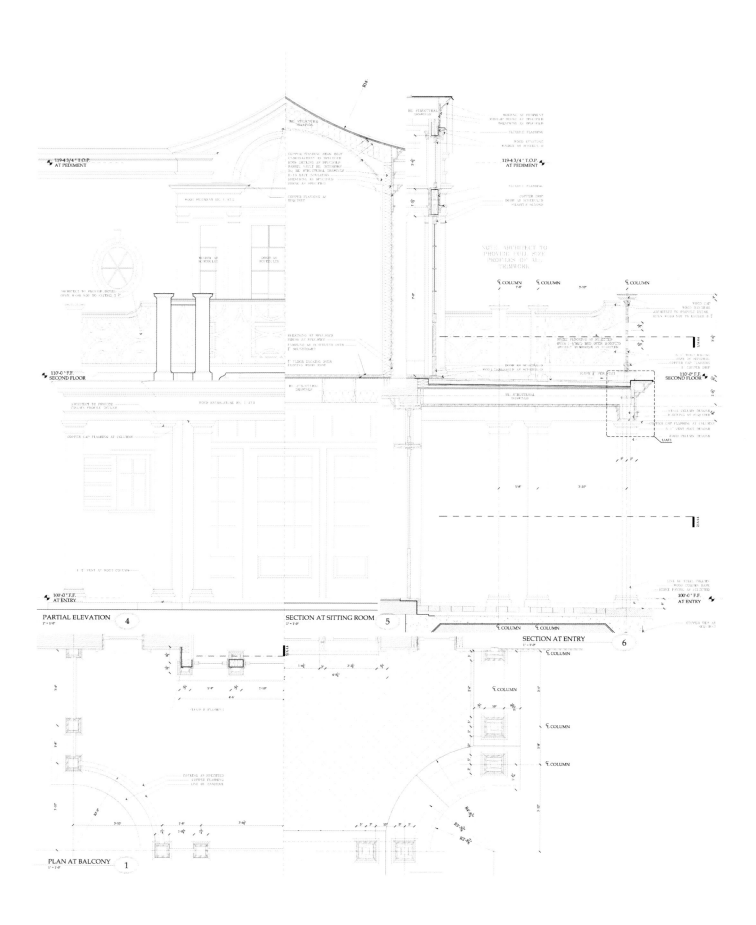

PARTIAL ELEVATION   4

SECTION AT SITTING ROOM   5

SECTION AT ENTRY   6

PLAN AT BALCONY   1

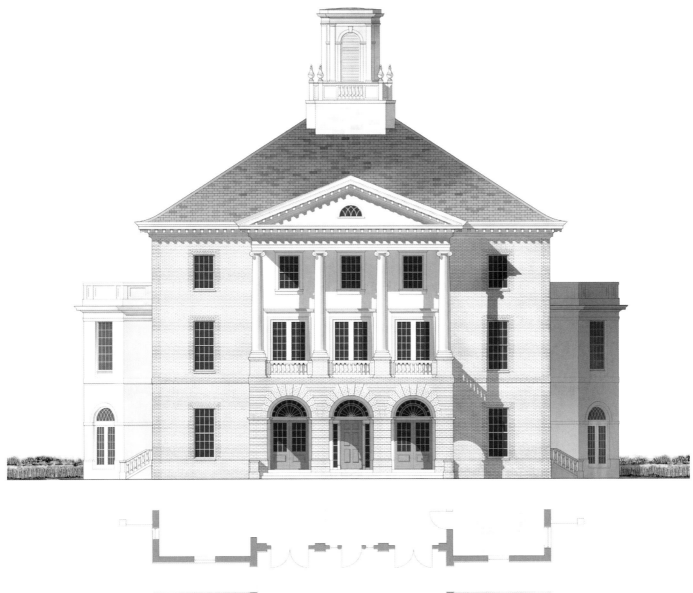

Left: An analytique demonstration of how construction documents such as plan, elevation, and section can be artfully arranged in one drawing. Roland Muñoz, *Home in Belaire, California*.

Above: A concise computer drawing illustrating the materiality of the brick on the façade of a fraternity headquarters in Columbus. Jim Lenahan, *Delta Gamma Headquarters Elevation*.

Previous spread: A detail of a rendering produced using a combination of hand drawing, watercolor and computer graphics. Jim Lenahan, *Delta Gamma Sorority, University of Arkansas*.

Right: Architectural template: plans, sections, and elevations with details of the main dome and minaret showing the earth-moon geometry on which the design was based. M. Hosuam Jiroudy, *Arch, Al Jaleel Mosque*.

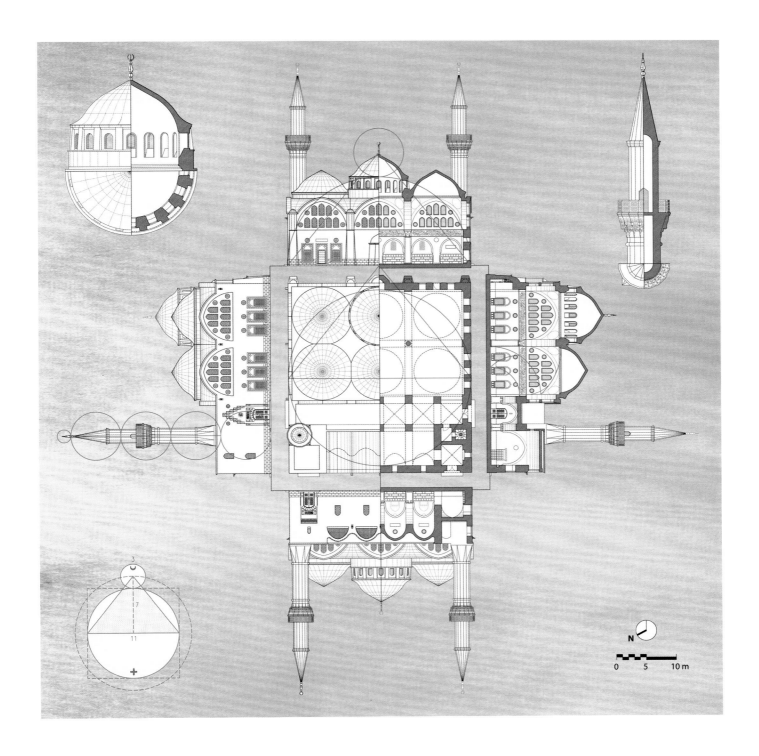

N

0   5   10 m

Town Quarry, Vinalhaven   Mel - '31

Maine Studio

"Truth in Nature"

John Ruskin, *Modern Painters*, 1894

As an architect, my intent is to continue to hone the ability to draw and to see. Travel has always been important in cataloging my many experiences. This is one hallmark of the architect's creative education and growth. We call it "recharging". Architects have also painted landscapes for generations to better hone their skill of observation and to learn the concepts of beauty from nature. Having a house on an island in Maine offered me a unique opportunity to experience and absorb an authentic American landscape and to explore an artistic interpretation of it through the eyes of the local culture.

After spending some time painting on porches and puzzle tables, I eventually built a studio, a controlled environment in which I could focus on capturing scenes of the coast with deeper thought and practice. Longer periods of time could be dedicated to understanding paint and its manipulation to capture a moment in time, or a quality of light. Robert Peabody writes of the sea as his inspiration, stating, "Certainly nowhere is nature so large, so direct, as on the sea." He quotes Byron in his sketchbook,

> *Ten thousand fleets sweep over thee in vain;*
> *Man marks the earth with ruin; his control*
> *Stops with the shore.*

The moods here change quickly: a fading light; a bright blue day suddenly becoming shrouded in a dense blanket of gray fog; a sudden squall or brilliant sunset; a bright blue mirror suddenly whipped up into furious waves; or a tide giving life to a craggy island but only temporarily before it disappears beneath the depth of the oceans waves once more. This landscape also takes on many characters throughout the seasons of spring, summer, fall, and winter; each offers a unique light and spirit.

A quick sketch of a quarry local to Michael's own cottage, done on rough cold press paper. Michael G. Imber, *Town Quarry*.

Summer bustles with activity. The long days start with lobster boats at 4 am—the rumbling of the engines drifting through an open window. From the porch we watch sailboats and sailing ships drift by on a soft sea breeze, and across the body of water known as The Reach, the chants of rowers in Bantry Bay gigs echo throughout Old Harbor as their oars, moving in unison, slap against the wood of their boats like a bass drum.

The long days of summer offer the chance to walk along a shoreline, or moor a boat in a hidden cove—an opportunity for *plein-air* painting. This is the moment to learn from nature, observing the purplish hue of a low fog on the horizon as it moves to envelop the landscape, a warm glow as it filters the afternoon sun; or the saturated hues of summer pooled in the moving tide. There is no better way to understand light; its reflection and refraction; how it defines and how it diffuses.

Winters are harsh and dark. A fire crackles all day long, and time can be spent laboring over a painting in the soft, warm light of the studio. Here, I can tackle larger paintings over the hours of the day, choosing my colors carefully and laying them down with intention. Days are short and the light rakes the landscape with long shadows, yet the light of the sea glows luminous, often frothy from chilled winds. What once was verdant green is now a deep burnt sienna or ochre, edged in black stone. One can awaken in the morning to a transformed landscape cloaked in a soft whiteness. A breaking storm can reveal a sharp sparkling scene streaked with purple and blue shadows.

Left: A demonstration of the precise definition that can be achieved on cold press paper. Michael likes to work with a range of materials including different papers, as it encourages awareness of medium. Michael G. Imber.

Right: Color moves completely differently on hot-pressed paper, becoming more fluid due to the smooth surface. Michael G. Imber, *Neglected Shoreline*.

The local town harbor near Michael's studio. Michael G. Imber,
Carver's Harbor.

Above: Capturing scenes of a harbor that is ever-changing. On this particular day the sea showed warmer tints of blue. A tall-masted boat is visible in the bay. Michael G. Imber, *Carver's Harbor*. 12 1/2" x 8 3/4".

Following spread: A study of the way light bounces off the water and reflects onto the rock, which is a piece of architecture in itself. Michael G. Imber, *Rock Island*.

A rendering on the smooth surface of hot press paper.
Michael G. Imber, *Carver's Harbor, Working Waterfront*.

The rocky outcrops along the Maine coastline are rich subjects for painting. The colors in the sky, the shadows on the rocks, and the ever-changing sea provide endless fuel for experimenting with watercolor. Michael G. Imber, *Crocketts Point, Vinalhaven Island, Maine*. Watercolor on hot press paper.

A large watercolor study of the different ways colors are blended.
Michael visited the site to sketch it before returning to the studio to
paint, everything being completed the same day. Michael G. Imber,
Tidal Pool, Vinalhaven, Maine, Lanes Island.

Hurricane Sound

This quick drawing of a fog bank rolling in on the old harbor in
front of Michael's house took less than an hour. Michael G. Imber,
Hurricane Sound. 12 ³/₄″ x 7 ¹/₄″.

A study of the boats that come into Camden Harbor. Michael G. Imber, *Camden Harbor*.

A study of the composition of boats and their relationship to the environment around them. The reflection was carefully observed. Michael G. Imber, *Camden Harbor*.

The fisherman's wharf in North Haven. Michael G. Imber, *Fishermans Wharf, North Haven, Maine*.

Teel Island   MGI·2022

A private island where N.C. Wyeth, his son, and grandson, would often paint. With Linda L. Bean's dory in the forground. Michael G. Imber, *Teel Island*.

Lanes Island

Previous spread: A large study of the Maine landscape on
watercolor paper. Great attention was paid to capturing the
movement of the clouds rolling across the sea. Michael G. Imber,
Lanes Island. 18 ³/₄″ x 9″.

Above: The harvesting of syrup from maple trees. Michael G. Imber,
Sugaring.

A clump of mossy birches outside Michael's studio. Michael G. Imber,
Birches At Squid Cove.

Left: A fir tree looks out across The Reach, in front of Michael's cottage. Working with the Whisky Watercolor Club has encouraged Michael to paint more frequently. Michael G. Imber, *Fir Tree overlooking The Reach*.

Above: Winter storm on Lanes Island in Maine. Michael G. Imber, *Lanes Island*.

Villa d'Este   5.13.18 M. appleton

Sketching Friendships

"'Do you sketch?' I do a little in that line myself, and we shall have no end of opportunities to exercise our skill."

John Calvin Stevens, *The Paintings of John Calvin Stevens*

Stevens and his Brush'uns enjoyed many days in the field sitting among the jagged rocks of the coast with a jigger of whisky and an umbrella to shade them from the sun. A similar love of painting brought together the Whisky Watercolor Club. Five architects—myself, Ankie Barnes of Washington, D.C., Thomas Kligerman of New York, Douglas Wright of New York, and Steve Rugo of Chicago—met through various professional organizations and became friends through travel and a love of watercolor. After painting together in England, a camaraderie, as with Stevens' Brush'uns, formed around sitting and painting together. Then, while traveling in India, the pandemic suddenly threatened to trap us abroad. As we each found safe routes home on some of the last flights back to the States, we vowed to continue painting together weekly while our offices went remote and we found ourselves in isolation. This formed a strong bond and friendship over architecture and painting alike.

Weekly exercises improved our skills of observation and control over capturing natural effects by brush and watercolor. Some exercises consisted of painting a past travel photograph or emulating the techniques of a master such as Homer's deep contrasting values; John Singer Sargent's bravado of the brush or his ability to capture the luminosity of a material; Andrew Wyeth's mixing of paint on paper; or Edward Hopper's use of color. These exercises would usually be an hour long as we painted together over our computer screens, yet sometimes would go on for hours, often with a whisky by our side, and long conversations about architecture and painting.

During lulls in the pandemic we would travel to meet up, sometimes all of us as a group, often just a couple of us, as time and our architectural practices allowed. Much like the Brush'uns, we would find ourselves painting landscapes in New Mexico, Montana,

Michael, Marc Appleton, and some other artistic friends went to a villa in Tivoli, Italy and spent the week there painting watercolors. Marc Appleton, *Villa d'Este*.

257

Devon in England, and of course on the rocky shores of New England. Sometimes these were hurried exercises of thirty, twenty, sometimes fifteen minutes of painting a scene *plein-air*, but most often lingering in a beautiful setting for hours absorbing its lessons. Finding ourselves sitting in a boat painting a coastal scene, or sitting in the hot desert sun painting a brilliant Southwest landscape, we learned to control the paint in both damp and dry conditions.

Happily, the Whisky Watercolor Club is not alone. There are other architects in this large, if shrinking, community of artist-architects: architects who view the work of an architect as a product of seeing the world through an artist's eye. Although there are Modernist architects, such as Steven Holl and James Cutler, and even radical Modernists such as Thom Mayne, who continue to use drawing and painting in their process of creating architecture, most of the architects today who avail themselves of this ancient tool are traditional architects following in the footsteps of those before in the continuation of a practice that architects have used since the 16th century. You see in their work a deeper understanding of the world of beauty. You see a nuance in their buildings' forms and compositions, and an eye for detail that goes well beyond two-dimensional appliqué. This is more than mere conceptualization; it is also seen in the final execution of their buildings. There is depth of understanding and articulation in their work that is rare among others.

All of this comes from the training of their eye and the ways they reveal and articulate their ideas. By drawing landscapes, by seeing and observing, their input is greater and their output more connected to the world as we see and experience it. I know of other artist-architects and I am sure there are more that I am not familiar with. My hope is that there are many more to follow.

Left: Michael spent more time painting watercolors like this during the Covid pandemic. This skull, from a shelf in Michael's studio, was an opportunity to practice form, perspective, and the way light hits an object. Michael G. Imber, *Rodent Relic*.

Right: A sketch of Whisky Watercolor Club member Thomas Kligerman painting in the courtyard of Goddards, Abinger Common in England. Michael G. Imber, *Painting at Goddards*.

There are many more architects today that have entered architecture through merely a lens of technology. As computers quickly became the tool of preference for the architect to produce their work, schools raced to adapt to a pedagogy and belief that architects no longer needed to be artists in order to vision the buildings of today. For that matter it was no longer necessary to even draw. This would introduce a whole new legion of young architects and technicians that knew only of the machine and the most recent software to produce their work. Indeed, they have found many new ways to expand the capabilities of technologies in building, and have explored form, space, and structure never before thought possible. But are we now lacking something of what it means to be an architect?

Architects have always been the medium between culture and nature. We have negotiated that which is natural and that which is man-made in order to arrive at a built environment from an understanding of both. Call it a reconciliation between nature and the nature of man. The art of the architect has always been a process of observing, interpreting, and envisioning through the language of the hand. It is the hand that has been the instrument of the mind, that which can instantly and fluidly express all that we have seen, and all that we have learned: all that we know. If, as architects, we lose our ability to draw—to see the world we live in through the eyes of an artist—will our buildings be left without the spirit of our humanity? Will our buildings be without an understanding of our place within nature? It is my suggestion that these are the questions AI will never be able to adequately answer.

Art is more than marks on canvas and on paper. It is an outward expression of who we are, both as individuals and as communities. It is what binds us in our beliefs, and in our understanding of who we are. It is our place in the world. As artists and as architects we must interpret our relationships with nature and with one another. It is always what it has meant to be an architect, and it has always been what it means to draw.

A painting exercise of a pair of barns, done with members of the
Whisky Watercolor Club. Michael G. Imber, *Yellow Barn*.

A Whisky Watercolor Club excercise from a photo of a window
nook. Michael G. Imber, *Nook*. 12 ¾" x 8 ¾".

Snow settled on an oak tree during a major snowstorm in San
Antonio. This was painted from a photograph by each member
of the Whisky Watercolor Club during their weekly video calls.
Michael G. Imber, *San Antonio Snowstorm*.

Mountain Hut

Another exercise done with the Whisky Watercolor Club, this time a depiction of a mountain scene. Michael G. Imber, *Mountain Hut*.

Although Michael and Ankie Barnes were sitting in front of the
same scene, their renderings are quite different. Ankie Barnes,
Browns Headlight.

Michael's version of the lighthouse. Different approaches to the
application of the paint: subtle interpretations of the landscape
are revealed. Michael G. Imber, *Browns Headlight*.

Chamisa   Santa Fe '21

The Whisky Watercolour Club finally got the chance to gather and paint together in Santa Fe during a remission in Covid lockdown restrictions. Michael G. Imber, *Chamisa, Sandia Mountains*.

Quarteles, New Mexico   mel 2021

Sketches became more rapid as the intensity of the sun grew later in
the day, and watercolours began evaporating off the brush almost
before they could be put to paper. Michael G. Imber, *Quarteles,
New Mexico.*

Sitting in the shimmering heat, members of the Whisky Watercolor
Club painted the Santo Cristo Mountains of New Mexico. Douglas
Wright, *Santa Fe*. Hot press 140lb paper, 11″ x 14″.

Across valleys and mountains. Steve Rugo, *Tesque, New Mexico*.
6" x 12".

Kligerman was experimenting with shadows, exaggerating the
blues and purples to create forms. "Shadows on a sunny day are
just the sky laying across the earth. You can paint shadows with
the same blue you use on the sky." Thomas Kligerman, *Mountains*,
2021. 7 ½" x 5 ⅛".

New Mexico   Ankie 2021

Dramatic blue shadows in New Mexico. Watercolor on cold pressed
300g/m² watercolor paper. Ankie Barnes, *New Mexico*.

An impressionistic painting of San Francisco de Asís Mission
Church in Ranchos de Taos, New Mexico. After applying the paint
with his brush, Kligerman stippled the wet surface with his fingertip
to create a more surreal interpretation. Thomas Kligerman, *Taos*,
2021. 5 ½″ x 5″.

Hills near Tesque, New Mexico. Ankie Barnes. Watercolor,
5 ¼″ x 8 ¼″.

A study of a bottle of whisky, inspired by the name of the
Whisky Watercolor Club. Light winks gently off its glass surface.
Douglas Wright, *Whisky Bottle*.

A street scenes with minimal visual information to allow the viewer
to complete the picture. Steve Rugo, *St Germaine aux Pres Paris*.
8 ½" x 8 ½".

Every artist has a unique interpretation of a scene. A waterfall painted dramatically from below. Michael G. Imber after Fritz Thaulow, *Haug Falls*. 8 ¾" x 6".

A different approach to capturing the light thrown off the water.
Douglas Wright after Fritz Thaulow, *Haug Falls*. Hot press 140lb
paper, 11″ x 14″.

Another view of the waterfall. Ankie Barnes after Fritz Thaulow, *Haug Falls*. Watercolor on cold pressed 300g/m² watercolor paper.

An attempt to feel the power of the water in an eastern mill town.
Steve Rugo after Fritz Thaulow, *Haug Falls*. 6″ x 8 ½″.

The challenge of painting architecture in watercolor is to keep the
building crisp and tectonic. This painting combines architecture
and landscape so there is a little more freedom in the cliffs. Thomas
Kligerman, *Petra*, 2020. 5 ¼″ x 8 ¼″.

Michael's interpretation of a famous archaeological site in Jordan's southwestern desert, where the architecture is carved out of the cliffs. Michael G. Imber, *Petra*.

A beautiful city scene from Siegle's travels in Italy.
Stephen Siegle, *Perugia*.

Another travel drawing capturing the majesty of St Mark's Basilica.
Stephen Siegle, *St Mark's Basilica*.

Left: A sketch in situ. Hatching captures the dramatic shadows between the pillars. Duncan McRoberts, *Tempietto*. Pen and ink, 8 ½" x 11".

Above: A freehand study. Duncan McRoberts, *S. Maria della Pace*.

A cathedral in Venice on the Punta della Dogana. It takes on the quality of a creature both outstretched and looming up toward you; the terracotta tail of the receding structures setting off the gray cathedral in the foreground with its two "eyes" giving it an even stronger anthropomorphized quality. McLean Jenkins: *Santa Maria della Salute*. Ink and watercolor on paper, 10" x 14".

Detail of a house in Scarsdale, NY. The focus of this detail was on
the strong diagonal of shadow and roof line, which gives the study
both a dynamic and abstract quality. McLean Jenkins, *Shadow Detail*.
Graphite, ink and watercolor on paper, 8″ x 8″.

A very quick painting with an emphasis on the high contrast between sunlit faces and shaded areas of the house and garden. When successful, these quick studies capture a sense of spontaneity and energy that a more detailed rendering often loses. McLean Jenkins, *Woolverstone House*. Ink and watercolor on paper, 9″ x 12″.

The interior of a club room in New York. Bill Curtis, *Luncheon at the
Salmagundi Club*. Watercolor on 140lb cold press cotton paper,
8" x 12".

Curtis saw the Whisky Watercolor Club's drawings of the oak
tree in San Antonio and wanted to do one of his own. Bill Curtis,
San Antonio winter. Watercolor on 140lb cold press cotton paper,
13 ½" x 10 ½".

A Sicilian street scene, brought to life by Cameron's atmospheric
watercolors. Richard Cameron, *Ragusa*. Watercolor and pencil on
rough watercolor paper, 8″ x 14″.

Expressive strokes capture the spacious, sunlit square.
Richard Cameron, *Piazza Navona*. Watercolor and pencil
on rough watercolor paper, 8″ x 14″.

This drawing of the Luxor Temple was a gift to Michael from Keith Summerhour. It hangs in Michael's office, commemorating their travels together in Egypt. Keith Summerhour, *Luxor Temple*.

The Art of the Architect

4.14.2015 Philae

Picture Credits

All artwork and photography © Michael G. Imber and Michael G. Imber, Architects except the following:

Front endpaper: © Sissy Martin
6: © Smithsonian American Art Museum, Bequest of Emily Finch Gilbert through Julia Post Bastedo, executor, 1962.13.36
10: © Abdel-Wahel El-Wakil
20: © George Knight
22: © Claudia Carle
24/25: © Max Baum
27: © Max Baum
28/29: © Max Kronauer
30: © National Gallery of Art, Washington, Gift of William B. O'Neal, 1987.73.2
32: © ETH Library Zurich, Old and Rare Prints, 10.7890/ethz-a-000462468
33: © Reproduced by courtesy of Abbot Hall, Lakeland Arts Trust, England
35: © Call Number (MS Typ 1096). Houghton Library, Harvard University
36: © Universal Images Group North America LLC / Alamy Stock Photo, PicturesNow / UGI
39 top: © Daniel J. Terra Collection, 1999.83. Terra Foundation for American Art, Chicago / Art Resource, NY
39 bottom: © National Gallery of Art, Washington, Gift of Frederick Sturges, Jr.,1953.1.1
40: © Art Institute Chicago, Friends of American Art Collection
41: © Brooklyn Museum, Museum Collection Fund and Special Subscription, 11.545
42/43: © Linda Bean's Maine Wyeth Gallery
44: © Smithsonian American Art Museum, Bequest of Helen Huntington Hull, granddaughter of William Brown Dinsmore, who acquired the painting in 1873 for "The Locusts," the family estate in Dutchess County, New York, 1977.107.1
45: © U.S. Department of the Interior Museum, INTR 03001
46: © National Gallery of Art, Washington, Corcoran Collection (Museum Purchase, Gallery Fund), 2014.79.10
47: © National Gallery of Art, Washington, Gift of Jo Ann and

Julian Ganz, Jr. in honor of John Wilmerding, 2004.99.1
48/49: © Collection of the McNay Art Museum, Mary and Sylvan Lang Collection
51: © 2023 Heirs of Josephine N. Hopper / Licensed by Artists Rights Society (ARS), NY. Digital image © Whitney Museum of American Art / Licensed by Scala / Art Resource, NY, 70.1292
52: © The Metropolitan Museum of Art, Gift of George A. Hearn, 1910, 10.64.5
53: © Plattsburgh State Art Museum, State University of New York, USA, Rockwell Kent Collection, Bequest of Sally Kent Gorton. All rights reserved. Digital image The State Hermitage Museum, St. Petersburg, Photography © The State Hermitage Museum / photo by Andrey Terebenin
54: © Julian Francis Abele Collection, The Architectural Archives, University of Pennsylvania
57: © BAC Library, Memorial Library Collection
58: © San Diego History Center, 91_18475
59: © Memorial Art Gallery of the University of Rochester: R. T. Miller Fund
60: © Private Collection. Digital Image The Cooley Gallery, Old Lyme, CT
61: © Florence Griswold Museum, Gift of the Hartford Steam Boiler Inspection and Insurance Company
62: © John Galen Howard Collection, Environmental Design Archives, UC Berkeley
64: © Julia Morgan Papers MS0010, Special Collections and Archives, California Polytechnic State University
65: © Lionel H. Pries Collection, University of Washington Libraries, Special Collections, UW24231z
67: John H. Kell, Sr., Courtesy of Jeremy Kell
68: © Private Collection
69: © Collection of John Calvin Stevens, III
70: © John H. Kell, Sr., Courtesy of Jeremy Kell
71: © John H. Kell, Sr., Courtesy of Jeremy Kell
72: BAC Library, Memorial Library Collection

Bibliography

Allen, Gerald and Richard Oliver. *Architectural Drawing: The Art and the Process*
(New York, 1981). Watson-Guptill Publications.

Battistini, Matilde. *Symbols and Allegories in Art* (Los Angeles, 2005). J. Paul Getty Museum.

Brown, Jane. *The Art and Architecture of English Gardens* (New York, 1989). Rizzoli.

Carpo, Mario. *The Second Digital Turn: Design Beyond Intelligence* (Cambridge, Mass., 2017).
MIT Press.

Denenberg, Thomas, Amy Kurtz Lansing and Susan Danly. *Call of the Coast: Art Colonies
of New England* (Portland, 2009). Portland Art Museum.

Descartes, René. *A Discourse on the Method*. Tr. Ian Maclean (Oxford, 2006).
Oxford University Press.

Fletcher, William Dolan. *John Taylor Arms, A Man For All Time* (Torrington, 1982).
The Easton Press.

Freudenheim, Leslie Mandelson. *Building with Nature: Roots of the San Francisco Bay Region
Tradition* (Salt Lake City, 1974). Peregrine Smith.

Gebhard, David and Deborah Nevins. *200 Years of American Architectural Drawing*
(New York, 1977). Watson-Guptill Publications.

Goodyear, Anne Collins (ed.). *This is a Portrait If I Say So: Identity in American Art,
1912 to Today* (New Haven, 2016). Yale University Press

Green, Tyler. *Emerson's Nature and the Artists: Idea as Landscape, Landscape as Idea*
(Munich, 2021). Prestel.

Guptill, Arthur. *Sketching and Rendering in Pencil* (New York, 1922). Pencil Points Press.
Republished by Forgotten Books, London, 2018.

Guptill, Arthur. *Color in Sketching and Rendering* (New York, 1935). Reinhold.

Hartman, George E. and Jan Cigliano. *Pencil Points Reader: A Journal for the Drafting Room
1920-1943* (New York, 2004). Princeton Architectural Press.

Hubbard, William. *Complicity and Conviction: Steps toward an Architecture of Convention*
(Cambridge, Mass., 1981). MIT Press.

Isaacson, Walter. *Leonardo Da Vinci* (New York, 2017). Simon & Schuster.

Komanecky, Michael. *Jamie Wyeth, Rockwell Kent and Monhegan* (Rockland, 2012).
Farnsworth Art Museum.

Lampugnani, Vittorio Magnago. *Architecture of the 20th Century in Drawings*
(New York, 1982). Rizzoli.

Morgan, Keith N. Shaping an American Landscape: The Art and Architecture of Charles A. Platt
(Hanover, 1995). Hood Museum of Art, Dartmouth College.

Nevins, Deborah and Robert A.M. Stern. *The Architect's Eye: American Architectural Drawings
from 1799-1978* (New York, 1979). Pantheon Books.

Nicoll, Jessica. *Abraham J. Bogdanove: Painter of Maine* (New York, 1997). Spanierman Gallery.

Ochsner, Jeffrey Karl. *Lionel H. Pries, Architect, Artist, Educator* (Seattle, 2007). University of Washington Press.

Oliver, Richard. *The Making of an Architect: 1881-1981* (New York, 1981). Rizzoli.

Oliver, Richard. *Bertram Grosvenor Goodhue* (Cambridge, Mass., 1983). MIT Press.

Payne, Edgar. *Composition of Outdoor Painting* (California, 1941). 7th ed. 2005. DeRu Fine Arts.

Peters, Lisa N. and William H. Gerdts. *Abraham J. Bogdanove: Monhegan Summers* (New York, 2001). Spanierman Gallery.

Piper, David. *The Illustrated History of Art* (London, 2004). Bounty Books.

Powell, Helen and David Leatherbarrow (eds.). *Masterpieces of Architectural Drawing* (New York, 1982). Abbeville Press.

Richardson, Margaret. *The Craft Architects* (New York, 1983). Rizzoli.

Robbins, Edward. *Why Architects Draw* (Cambridge, Mass., 1977). MIT Press.

Ruskin, John. *The Elements of Drawing* (New York, 1971). Dover Publications.

Scully, Vincent. *The Architecture of the American Summer: The Flowering of the Shingle Style* (New York, 1989). Rizzoli.

Stamp, Gavin. *The Great Perspectivists* (New York, 1982). Rizzoli.

Steil, Lucien. *Tradition & Architecture: Palaces, Public Buildings & Houses* (New York, 1987). St. Martin's Press.

Stevens II, John Calvin and Earle G. Shettleworth, Jr. *John Calvin Stevens: Domestic Architecture 1890-1930* (Maine, 1990). Greater Portland Landmarks.

Stevens, Paul S. and Earle G. Shettleworth, Jr. *The Paintings of John Calvin Stevens* (Maine, 2015). Greater Portland Landmarks.

Sussman, Ann and Justin Hollander. *Cognitive Architecture: Designing for How We Respond to the Built Environment* (Abingdon, 2015). Routledge.

Winter, Robert. *Toward a Simpler Way of Life: The Arts & Crafts Architects of California* (Berkeley, 1997). University of California Press.

Acknowledgments

Although this book is an American story, it must be said that my early work was heavily influenced by English books such as Gavin Stamp's *The Perspectivists*, Margaret Wilson's *The Craft Architects*, and Jane Brown's *The Art and Architecture of English Gardens*. The story is incomplete without mentioning the great artist-architect traditions of Great Britain where drawings, used to present architectural proposals to clients, delved deep into the world of art, and mirrored the art world in its outlook on our relationship with the landscape. Artists such as Joseph Gandy, William Walcot, and even Sir Edwin Lutyens served as inspiration. To pursue a deeper dialog on these and other important architects would be another endeavor entirely.

The book is the result of a series of talks, first on my work, then on the influences in my work that led to a focus on art and landscape and its role in architecture. These talks included a lecture at the University of Notre Dame's symposium on Drawing in Architecture, *The Art of Architecture: Hand-drawing and Design* as well as talks for the American Institute of Architects and the Institute of Classical Architecture, among many others.

My knowledge of, and interest in, art are not academic, but that of a curious professional, limited to reading about and visiting numerous galleries, exhibits, and collections on the artists I mention. My time in Washington, D.C. saw me spending many long lunch hours in the National Gallery, Corcoran Museum, and other great collections of American artists. And my time in New England, and summers in Maine, brought me closer to the work of the artists of the Hudson River School, the Luminists, and the Cornish and New York Schools art colonies among others that paved the way for the work of the great Modern Regionalists that followed. I wish to thank Wyeth collector Linda Bean for her generosity and passion for all things Wyeth, as well as historians Jeffrey Karl Oshner, D.W Granston III and Earle G. Shettleworth Jr. for their endless resources.

This book has been fostered by the support of numerous people throughout the years. I wish to thank Professors Don Hanlon and Robert Ritter for their support of a student that went his own way. My first apprenticeship in Connecticut brought me close to several talented young architects, primarily Joeb Moore (now teaching at both Columbia University and at Yale) who urged me to sketch every single day. Allan Greenberg was as much a teacher as he was an employer. He fostered a thirst for learning that spawned an entire new generation of teachers of young architects.

Educating the next generation of architects is central to both this book and my own career. My relationships and time as a visiting critic and speaker at the College of Architecture at Notre Dame, as well as my teaching graduate design studio at the Yale School of Architecture, have only served to deepen my own understanding of the importance of drawing in architecture and the need to maintain the practice as a valued tool of the profession. I wish to thank Dean Michael Lykoudis,

Duncan Stroik, and Lucien Steil among others at Notre Dame for their strong belief in drawing and allowing me to be a part of their academic community and, of course, Dean Deborah Burke, Bob Stern, and George Knight of Yale for fostering an outside practitioner's voice on the importance of drawing and representational design. I owe George Knight, my associate professor, a debt of gratitude for his ever-erudite enthusiasm and support.

As an architectural studio Michael G. Imber, Architect has never stood alone. My vision for an architectural office that valued drawing, art, the landscape and culture and saw the value in a continuum of traditional practice in architecture was supported by many. My partner Mac White has been there from nearly the beginning, committed to our ethos of drawing and helping to attract other highly gifted individuals to the office who are passionate in art and in architecture. Many endlessly talented young architects have contributed greatly as they came through our studio, and several are mentioned in the body of this book.

There are numerous professional colleagues that have supported my pursuits, too many to thank all of them. But I cannot avoid naming the stars of the Whisky Watercolor Club: Ankie Barnes, Thomas Kligerman, Steve Rugo, and Douglas Wright. Their friendship and support on our travels together, and many weekends watercoloring, have only bolstered my learning and enthusiasm in painting. Stephen Harby and Marc Appleton must also be mentioned for our painting adventures in Italy, and thank you to Andres Duany for our inclusion on his *charrettes* in so many wonderful places.

Of course I would be remiss without thanking my family: Maxwell, Sari, and most of all my wife Mariann, for their patience for the long hours I have spent in my studio laboring over a painting, staring at a subject while a conversation fell on the deaf ears of someone focused on composition, color, and line, or waiting while I stopped to sketch mid-stride in the course of our travels. Without the support, encouragement and the criticisms only loved ones can give, I would not have the voice I have today.

Sissy Martin proved tenacious at tracking down copyrights. A final thanks to Clive Aslet for his never-ending enthusiasm for the subject of the book and for his devotion to having this book written in proper English.

A conceptual watercolor sketch for a garden pavilion done during a
charrette in Florida. Michael Imber, *Zen Pavilion, Windsor.*

First published in the United Kingdom in 2023 by Triglyph Books.

Triglyph Books
154 Tachbrook Street
London SW1V 2NE

www.triglyphbooks.com
Instagram: @triglyphbooks

Designed by Steve Turner
www.steveturnerdesign.com

Publisher: Clive Aslet and Dylan Thomas
Production Manager: Kate Turner
Production Coordinator: Claire Mercer
Assistant Editor: Ines Cross
Editorial Assistant: Leona Crawford
Copyeditor and proofreader: Mike Turner

British Library Cataloguing-in-Publication Data.
A catalogue record for this book is available from the British Library.

ISBN: 978-1-9163554-9-1

Printed and bound sustainably in Italy.

THE ART OF
THE ARCHITECT

TRIGLYPH
BOOKS